Leonard Arthur's

Thoughts and Revelations

on

The EU

Read before you vote

PREFACE

In the run-up to the 2016 referendum on Great Britain leaving the EU I had the feeling that we should separate. Perhaps it was age as I approached my 79th birthday, or the feelings of distrust that has increasingly come to me of politicians in general. I say in general because it would be wrong to discredit all politicians. As someone once said "It is only the 95% of politicians that give the rest a bad name".

Why had I come to distrust politicians. Memory is, perhaps, notoriously unreliable but mine tells me that in my early days of political awareness politicians were usually ex military, ex judiciary, ex academics, with some from the performing arts. From the more socialist areas there were some from the working class background, but my overall feeling was that they people first and politicians second, almost amateurs in the game. Then sometime later, about the 1950's or 60's I began to hear phrases such as "We need more professional politicians, who should be paid accordingly". "Professional government requires well paid professional people". This set in motion the trend for what we have reached today. Increasing numbers of bright young things; products of the university streams that taught politics, economics, the classics and history. And, for me, this it where it began to go wrong. Not that there is anything wrong with a high level education. But, for me, the path from university into the life of a political analyst, aide to an existing politician, political strategist, or any of those early steps, is missing the most vital of elements, an understanding of life in the reality.

My feeling is that politics became less of a profession and more of a job. Some people are lucky, in that they find a job that provides them with genuine job satisfaction. A few, perhaps, if offered a job with more money but less job satisfaction, might stay in the job they are in. But, in my experience, particularly as consumerism has become the religion of the day, most see the job as a way of making money and increasing that money is the overwhelming objective. So now I no longer see politicians as people apart, who nobly strive to improve the well being of their constituents, well! a miniscule number might, but the most are just like us. It is a job. "Give me the chance to become richer and I will take it".

In the run-up to the referendum two main issues seemed to be the most prevalent. Restoring national sovereignty, in order to control immigration. The second was the economic impact of leaving the EU. One side seemed to say we are in danger of being overrun by foreigners, while the other said that leaving the EU would bankrupt the country. To me neither of these was credible. I believe immigration is a problem whether we are in the EU or not. I also believe that politicians have surrendered control to the money markets, they react to changes caused by the markets and do not have much control of how those markets operate. Consequently, the economy will be subject to fluctuations, whether or not we remain in the political EU.

Note that I used the word "political" as a preface to the title EU. My problem is with the political EU. I want to see a European economic bloc that can rival any of the other world trading groups. This I will support, and campaign for. It is the political element that causes me to fret. So, I investigated this political EU and came to the conclusion I was right to be suspicious. I now want to make this information known as widely as possible, because there are people, with vested interest, who want to see the wishes of the referendum reversed.

If there is going to be a second referendum I would like people to know exactly what sort of institutions they are faced with. Please bear in mind these are my thoughts and feelings. Read and consider, then also consider the other options. Most of all, if there is to be another vote, please vote with some knowledge of the wider issues and not on prejudice or single issues.

In this document I will give a brief overview of the institutions of the EU and a number of its support agencies. I want people to fully understand just how vast the EU is and then to decide for themselves whether this is the sort of European supranational organisation they want.

Then if there has to be another referendum on the UK relationship with Europe they can vote with a greater knowledge of the political EU. This, first section, is not meant to be read in detail it is intended to show just how big the structural elements of the EU are and to show how many Presidents, Vice Presidents, Commissioners,

Director Generals, Secretary Generals and so on, through the whole gamut of staffing levels.

Most of the information comes from EU websites. The main one is Europa.eu. A second major site is EU.whoiswho. They will give you entry into the EU and its people. Of course there are many other option, just enter "EU agencies" into your browser and all can be found. I urge you to explore and find out just how vast this organisation is and how far it has come from its original concept "The Common Market". Then if a second referendum is to take place you will have some knowledge of just what this Political EU is and you can vote with that knowledge in mind.

The listed main institutions of the EU are the:
- European Parliament
- European Council
- Council of the European Union
- European Commission
- Court of Justice of the European Union
- European Central Bank
- European Court of Auditors
- European External Action Service.

Lesser institutions are the:
- Committee of the Regions
- European Economic and Social Committee
- Consultative Committee on Industrial Change
- European Anti-Fraud Office
- EU Inter-Institutional Bodies.

In some cases I have examined the structure and listed the upper level and middle management positions. These sections are not intended for detailed reading. They are intended for the reader to browse through and gain an insight into the large number of positions that exist in these EU bodies, and the, seemingly, repetitive nature of work across the bodies. Almost every institution has a department concerned with "EU Enlargement". The Washington Post correspondent, Tom Reid commented "Nobody would have deliberately designed a government as complex and redundant as the EU".

I ask you to read on and gain an insight into this "Political" EU and if there is to be another public vote ask yourself, "Is this the sort of organisation I want to say yes to."

THE EU PARLIAMENT

The EU website indicates that there are seven main institutions to its structure. One of these is the EU parliament and it is described as the "first institution" of the EU. According to the EU's own website this "first" title is because it has ceremonial precedence over all the other institutions. The word ceremonial gives the clue because, in fact, the parliament does not have legislative initiative power. Legislation is initiated by the European Commission and sent to the parliament and the European Council for approval. The parliament is, supposedly, equal with the council in this respect, except that there are specific legislative issues where the council does not have to have the support of the parliament.

What makes the parliament unique is that it is the only institution that has fully democratically elected members. The people of Europe can have a say, every five years, on who they send to the parliament. The other institutions compile short lists for the senior positions within those institutions, which are sometimes sent to the parliament for approval. The referral to parliament for approval is not always the case, but more of that later.

Parliament Structure.
At the time of this compilation the parliament comprises:
- 750 voting members
- one President, who does not vote
- 14 Vice Presidents
- 25 Committees

- 44 Delegations.

I could at this stage go into great detail about the above elements of the parliament, but this would lead into endless detail which could bore the reader. Remember this is just one of the major seven institutions and the above numbers give some idea of just how big this one institution is. If you would like to see the details just go to the EU website – europa.eu and look at the individual institutions for the detailed breakdown.

Parliament Sites.
- Strasbourg
- Brussels
- Luxembourg.

The primary parliamentary site is at Strasbourg, but the parliament only meets there for one week each month, well actually only four working days each month because the members have to uproot from Brussels and travel in chartered trains to Strasbourg and back again. Take the travelling time out and, at most, only four work days result. Most parliamentary sessions take place at Brussels, which is the secondary site. So, why is this? The answer is, in part, Luxembourg, which is the home of the EU parliament Secretariat. All the administration for the parliament is done from Luxembourg. Because Brussels and Luxembourg are near neighbours it makes sense to have meetings where the parliament and its secretariat are closest. Also the Commission and Council are in these locations. Then, why bother with

Strasbourg? Well, this is where you begin to see the structural dysfunction of the political EU.

The current EU parliamentary structure grew out of the 1952 European Coal and Steel Community. In 1962 it gave birth to the European Parliament, which then was made up of seconded members of the national country parliaments. In 1979 direct elections were held to create the Members of the European Parliament (MEP's) as independent individuals.

When the EU sets up any institution, it likes to share the responsibilities between as many member states as possible. In the past Strasbourg has been an issue between Germany and France so it was decided that, to please both countries, Strasbourg would be the primary parliamentary seat. To give Luxembourg something it was decided that the Secretariat would be there. The distance between the parliament and its secretariat soon became an issue, so finally, because Belgium was seen as something like a neutral EU, de-facto, capital city and was close to Luxembourg, a secondary parliament was established there.

So we currently have the ridiculous situation where each month trains are chartered to take MEP's from Brussels to Strasbourg, with plastic bins (cantines) of documents and the necessary support staff to hold sessions in the Strasbourg seat. The session is only for four days, the Friday is for travelling back, but, MEP's are allowed to claim their €300 attendance allowance for sitting in an air conditioned train and enjoying the ride. Road transport is also needed to take other materials. And, not only does the Parliament move, but the Commission also has to make the journey because, as stated, the Parliament has no legislative authority so the Commission must be present to give the Parliament legislative credibility.

This arrangement is not even popular with most MEP's. It is alleged that 89% of MEP's would support a single seat parliament, but they do not have the power to make it happen. The EU Commission decides policy and even if they were to want to change the current situation there is a problem. The Strasbourg seat was ratified by the 1992 Summit meeting at Edinburgh, which was agreed, and signed off by all, the then, national political heads of state. To make a change would require the heads of state to agree, and, when he was President of France, Nicholas Sarkozy declared that the question of changing the status of the Strasbourg seat was non-negotiable. The mayor of Strasbourg has also declared that he would make things very difficult for the EU if they attempt to change the status of his city. So it seems that the great EU idea of a global European democracy can fail when narrower national interest is concerned.

The cost of running this crazy parliamentary set-up has been calculated at €1.2 billion per annum. Currently, that is four times that of the UK parliament. The EU's own Court of Auditors has calculated that savings of €113.8 million per year could be made by having a single seat parliament. A parliamentary study put the cost of the extra seat at €200 million, and added that the current travel between the two seats created 20,268 tonnes of carbon dioxide emissions (so much for the EU high moral stance on greenhouse gas reduction).

While on the subject of costs, because every MEP has the right to address the parliament in his own language it is necessary for the parliament to employ 350 full time translators, with a further 400 part time translators. Languages include such divisions as Basque, Catalan, Valencian and Galician. A 2006 report stated that the daily cost of translation was €118,000, which could be reduced to €8,900 per day if a set number of core languages could be introduced.

The EU Parliament Secretariat

The EU parliament secretariat comprises the following directorates each of which is headed by a Director General. Below him each directorate has up to five Directors, but most have four. This means that there are thirteen Director Generals and more than 52 Directors in this one part of just one of the seven main EU institutions.

- Directorate General for the Presidency
- Directorate-General for Internal Policies of the Union
- Directorate-General for External Policies of the Union
- Directorate-General for Parliamentary Research Services
- Directorate-General for Communication

- Directorate-General for Personnel
- Directorate-General for Infrastructure and Logistics
- Directorate-General for Translation
- Directorate-General for Logistics and Interpretation for Conferences
- Directorate-General for Finance
- Directorate-General for Innovation and Technological Support
- Directorate-General for Security
- Legal Service.

Again, I will not go into detail. If you wish to expand your knowledge you may go to the EU website and search for the Secretariat of the EU parliament. There you will find the complete breakdown of personnel, together with a thumbnail photograph, and you can even investigate the CV of individuals. One of the best sites on the EU domain is "europa.eu/whoiswho". This gives the complete list of all the EU institutions and by clicking on any one it will open up that institution and give the complete hierarchy.

THE COUNCILS OF THE EU

When the word "Council" appears we have to be careful about which part of the EU, or not, that we are referring to. The European Council should not be confused with the "The Council of the EU," which is another EU institution, or "The Council of Europe" which is another body, not part of the EU.

The European Council

The European Council is made up of the heads of state of all member countries of the EU, plus a president of the European Council and the president of the European Commission. Its primary purpose is to define the overall political direction and priorities of the EU. Other functions of the European Council are to:

- elect the president of the Council
- propose the president of the Commission
- appoint the High Representative of the Union for Foreign Affairs and Security Policy
- officially appoint the body of Commissioners
- appoint the Executive Board of the European Central Bank (ECB), including its president.

The European Council is scheduled to meet four times each year. These meetings are usually referred to as "Summit Meetings". As stated the principal attendees are the national, or political, heads of state of the member countries, plus the Council President and the President of the Commission. Other specific individuals may be invited to attend where expert guidance may be needed in specific issues. Special meetings can be convened for more immediate concerns. For example, terrorist attacks where the EU may wish to take collective action against states who may be involved. Such a case was the aircraft attacks on the New York tower buildings. Presently a number of extra summit meetings are being called to negotiate Brexit.

The council has no formal legislative power but can provide input to guide the legislative policy of the EU. It may also be required to settle contentious issues, on collective foreign policy for example. The ratification of important documents, such as treaties, requires the approval of the council, and any changes to treaties must be agreed by the council.

On each issue, the European Council can, either request the Commission to make a proposal or pass the issue on to the Council of the EU for them to deal with.

The Council of the EU (Council of Ministers)
The Council of the EU is also referred to as the Council of Ministers. The Council of the EU has no fixed membership. When it meets it may be in any one of ten different subject configurations, therefore, it will comprise ministers from the member countries who are competent in the subject matter.

The functions of the Council of the EU are to:
- negotiate and adopt new EU laws which are based on proposals received from the Commission. It does this together with the EU parliament.
- coordinate the EU member countries policies
- develop EU foreign policy and security policy
- conclude agreements between the EU and other countries or organisations
- adopt the EU annual budget.

The configurations in which the Council of Ministers will meet are:
- Agriculture and Fisheries
- Competiveness
- Economic and Financial affairs
- Environment
- Employment, Social policy, Health and Consumer affairs
- Education, Youth Culture, and Sport
- Foreign affairs
- General affairs
- Justice and Home affairs
- Transport, Telecommunications and Energy.

The Council of Europe has no single president. The presidency rotates between member states on a six-monthly basis, therefore a representative of the country that currently holds the presidency will chair the council meetings. Because the six month presidency is short a tripartite system has been introduced. The current presidency may be assisted by the previous incumbent country, and the country which is next due to hold the presidency is given the opportunity to gain experience. This ensures a smoother transition between the office holders after such a short period of holding that office. But, it also triples, at least, the number of personnel in the presidency meetings and the associated costs will be hugely increased.

The General Secretariat of the Council of the EU (GSC)

The two council institutions share an administrative organisation, the General Secretariat of the Council (GSC). Since the European Council may meet only four times each year its administration is handled by this body.

The secretariat helps with the organisation of the councils' work. It assists the European Council and its president and also supports the council presidency in negotiations within the council and with the other EU institutions. It also provides logistical support and practical organisation of meetings (including meeting rooms, document production and translation).

When necessary, the GSC also handles the practical organisation of high-level meetings with heads of state and government or ambassadors from non-EU countries. Providing, as needed, draft agendas, reports, notes and minutes of meetings at all levels

The Secretariat is headed by a Secretary General who oversees a number of Directorates each headed by a Director General. The Directorates are:
- Directorate General - Economic Affairs and Competiveness
- Directorate General - General and Institutional policy.
- Directorate General - Justice and Home Affairs
- Directorate General - Legal Service
- Directorate General - Agriculture, Fisheries, Social Affairs and Health

- Directorate General - Foreign Affairs, Enlargement and Civil Protection
- Directorate General - Environment, Education, Transport and Energy
- Directorate General - Communications and Information
- Directorate General – Organisational Development and Services
- Directorate General - Digital Services.

To assist the secretariat it has a Committee of Permanent Representatives, who are spread across the 28 member states. A search of the EU "who's- who" website indicates that each permanent representative office has four members, at least.

Furthermore, the secretariat can call upon more than 150 highly specialised working parties and committees, named as Preparatory Bodies, -with more ad-hoc committees if extra specialisations are needed. Detailed information is available on all of the assisting bodies on the EU website and for the jargon title lovers it is quite revealing, and not without, perhaps unintended, humour. One of the preparatory bodies rejoices under the title "Horizontal Working Party on Drugs."

The Secretariat's own web site gives figures for 2018 that show it employed 2,770 staff. The financial breakdown showed it had a budget of €572.9 million, 61.6% of which was for staffing costs. At this point I have to say that the EU is totally transparent and, with sufficient research, in-depth information is available.

Perhaps they rely upon the fact that turn-out for the EU direct elections is below 50% and in some specific cases they show it as low as 28%. With so little interest maybe people will not be too inquisitive about the costs of this ever growing organisation.

As an idea of how the GSC organisation is structured the following shows the elements of the Secretary Generals Office:

- Secretary General
- Head of Private Office
- Director of Counter Terrorism Coordination
- Director of Task Force for the UK
- Head of Unit, Internal Audit
- Senior Administrator, Internal Audit
- Head of Unit, Data Protection.

Then there are the 10 Directorates, listed above, and an example structure of just one follows.

- Director Economic Affairs and Competitiveness
  - Head of Unit, Economic Policy
  - Head of Unit, Financial Affairs
  - Head of Unit , Budget and Financial Regulations
  - Head of Unit, Tax Policy. Export Credits and Regional Policy
  - Head of Unit, Internal Market, Consumer Policy, Better Regulations
  - Head of Unit, Competition, Customs-Union, Company law, Intellectual Property, Public Procurement

- Head of Unit, EU2020, Industry, Space, Research, Innovation.

All Directorates follow the same pattern, with a Director who oversees a number of Units each with a Head. In some cases there is a step below the Unit which is a Sector, again with a Sector Head. The site does not go further in showing how many people work in the Units and Sectors but, as indicated above the Secretariat has a staffing level of 2,770.

THE COMMISSION

The EU commission comprises the college of commissioners, one from each member country. From these, currently, 28 commissioners the following will be appointed:
- The President of the Commission
- 1st. Vice President
- Vice President and High Representative for foreign aid and security policy
- 4 other Vice Presidents.

(At this point the question may be asked, "how is it that the United States of America gets by with 1 President and 1 Vice President when the Unites States of Europe has multiple Presidents and Vice Presidents in its individual institutions).

Although the college of commissioners is representative of each member state they have to put aside their national identity in favour of the EU. When appointed the Commissioner has to take an oath of office, sworn before the European Court of Justice. Part of this oath puts the EU before any national interest and is shown below.

> "I solemnly undertake: to respect the Treaties and the Charter of Fundamental Rights of the European Union in the fulfilment of all my duties; to be completely independent in carrying out my responsibilities, in the general interest of the Union; in the performance of my tasks, neither to seek nor to take instructions from any Government or from any other institution, body, office or entity; to refrain from any action incompatible with my duties or the performance of my tasks."

So the Commission, which is the legislative body of the EU, and is unelected, makes rules within a framework which is isolationist.

The Commission is the real powerhouse of the EU. It is the EU executive body and it decides the political and strategic direction that the EU will take. Its stated, current list, of priorities are:

- Jobs growth and investment
- A digital single market
- Energy union and climate
- The internal market
- Deeper and fairer economic and monetary union

- A balanced and progressive trade policy to harness globalisation
- Justice and fundamental rights
- Migration
- Becoming a stronger global actor
- Democratic change.

Obviously with such an ambitious programme an administrative structure is needed and, like other EU institutions, the commission has risen to the challenge and created 53 departments and agencies to carry out its work. Twenty four of these are the Directorates General and, as we have seen, there will a number of Director Generals in each department, supervising an even greater number of directors. If you wish to examine these departments just go to the European Commission web page and click on the link "Composition" and all will be revealed.

Just as revealing is an investigation of the statistics on the commission staff. These web pages provide two very detailed Pie Charts for the year beginning 2018. These charts provide information on the employees in the commission, including number of personnel by gender, general job divisions and age. The total number of Commission staff is given as 32,196. Remember this is just one of the seven main institutions. There are still five lesser institutions to consider. Then we have agencies, delegations, ambassadors and special representatives. Overseeing the administrative arm of the Commission is the Secretary General's office, which wields considerable power and influence.

Back to the commission! The pie charts also reveal data, such as the managerial staff numbers include:

- 371 Senior managers
- 1,100 Middle managers

In the non-management grades there are:

- 11,463 Advisers
- 58 Special Advisers
- 7,161 Contract staff.

In the age data there are 10,059 personnel in the age range 50 – 59. Why is this relevant? Well, the EU pension data for 2017 indicated that the pension liability had reached a figure of €67.7 Billion (yes Billion). The Commission, alone, will, potentially, be contributing another 10,000 retirees over the next ten years so that pension liability is likely to increase, exponentially, in future years. We constantly hear in the news media how pension funds for organisations will have funding problems in the future. The EU pension fund will have to be funded by the European taxpayers to an extraordinary level in the years to come.

The Commission is often accused of being autocratic and secretive in some of its dealings. It has a history of such accusations and is currently mired in a controversy that confirms the worst fears on its political behaviour. The case concerns the appointment of a new Secretary General (SG) to the Commission. Remember the SG is the most senior administrator. The facts given below are a précis of the EU Ombudsman's report, following complaints regarding the appointment. If you wish to see the full report, go to the EU website and find the Ombudsman's site. Then enter Joint case 488/2018/KR & 514/2018/KR.

In 2015 the, then, SG, Mr. Italianer, told the President, Mr. Jean-Claude Juncker, that he would retire in 2018. Mr. Juncker determined that his, then, private office Chief of Staff, Mr Martin Selmayr would be the next SG. However, Mr. Selmayr was not part of the Secretariat and it was the usual practice that that the SG position would be filled by an existing Deputy Secretary/Director General, from one of the 24 Directorates of the Commission. At that time the President did not openly publish the fact that Mr. Italianer was to retire. He did, however, confide in Mr Selmayr, presumably to prepare him for what was to follow.

Move forward to 2018. In January a Deputy Secretary General position became available. Mr. Selmayr and one other candidate were put forward for the position. This second candidate withdrew, for reasons unknown, leaving only the President's preferred man. The next series of events are taken from the Ombudsman's report in the form of a time line:

- 08.39 - Feb. 21st. Mr. Italianer sent a formal letter to Mr. Juncker stating that he would retire on March 1st.
- 09.35 – Feb. 21st. At a meeting of the College of Commissioners Mr. Selmayr was appointed as a

Deputy Secretary General to the Commission Secretariat.
- Immediately following, Mr. Italianer told the College that he was stepping down from the SG post, something that was not put into the agenda of the meeting,
- Immediately following Mr. Selmayr was proposed as the next SG and the College approved Mr. Selmayr's appointment as the new Secretary General.
- 10.30 – Feb. 21st. Mr. Juncker announces the appointment of Mr. Selmayr as the new Secretary General from March 1st.

In this extraordinary sequence of affairs Mr. Selmayr had gone through two senior promotions in the space of a few minutes. The whole procedure, from the formal letter of resignation from the incumbent, to the public announcement of his successor took just under two hours. In the first promotion case Mr. Selmayr was un-apposed, following the withdrawal of the only other candidate, and in the second no other candidates had even a chance of being put forward.

Following complaints to the Ombudsman an enquiry was held and the conclusions stated there had been four instances of maladministration. These were:
- A failure to avoid a conflict of interest,
- A failure of the Consultative Committee for Appointments to act within rules,
- Holding a selection procedure which did not achieve its stated purpose,

- The impending retirement of Mr. Italianer was kept secret to, artificially, create a situation of urgency to fill the Secretary General post.

The official report goes into much more detail on the failings of the Commission. It covers some 50 pages and makes revealing reading. It was critical of the Commission, saying that when concerns were raised about the double promotion the Commission acted in an evasive, defensive and legalistic manner.

What is not included in the report is what action is to be taken. Any business conducting itself in this way would face some sort of sanction. But, it seems the EU autocrat is totally unaccountable and can make up the rules to suit themselves. It is not within the remit of the Ombudsman to make such sanctions. The Parliament has some power, in that it can call for a motion of "no confidence" in the Commission, but herein there is a problem. The MEP position is, probably the least secure in the EU, in that they may not be re-elected. Consequently, many MEP's have the objective of securing a more permanent EU position. Since many of those positions are by appointment, to be critical of the Commission will not help to make a move to a permanent post. For example, Mr. Nigel Farage, given his frequent criticism of the Commission, is unlikely to become a Commissioner. The Parliament has only once come close to its censure of the Commission and that was in 1998 when the threat of censure caused the resignation of the whole college. More on that later.

The Ombudsman's report has recommended that changes be made to the selection of candidates and the procedure for promotions. But, such things have happened before and by the time proposed changes have been through the discussion and committee stages they can be in a much reduced state. Real change is something that is difficult to bring to this political EU.

THE COURT OF JUSTICE OF THE EU

The EU Court of Justice is, in fact, two courts. The two courts differ only in the level at which they function. The courts are the Court of Justice and the General Court. These courts should not be confused with the European Court of Human rights, which not an EU institution. The administrative needs of the courts are dealt with by the Departments of the Court,

Overall the role of the EU courts is stated as, to:
- Ensure EU law is interpreted and applied the same in every EU country,
- Ensure countries and EU institutions abide by EU law,
- Settle legal disputes between national governments and EU institutions.

The Court of Justice
The Court of Justice operates at the national level and tends to provide preliminary rulings that emanate from the national courts of the EU countries. It will also make judgements on actions for appeals and annulment.

As a court it comprises a Judge from each of the member states, with Advocates to assist those judges. Obviously any legal procedure is not quite as simple as having just two functionaries so an investigation of the total composition is needed to have an understanding of the total structure of this institution. A search of "who-is-who" in the EU website reveals that the Court of Justice comprises the following:

- A President,
- Head of Private Office,
- Vice president,
- Head of Private Office,
- 7 Readers of Judgements,
- 9 Presidents of the Chamber,
- First Advocate General,,
- 11 Advocates General,
- 28 Judges,
- 111 Legal Secretaries,
- Registrar
- Deputy Registrar
- 2 Attaches to the Registrar.

Beneath these, of course, there are supporting staff and it is not unusual that the services of additional Advocates and Legal Secretaries may be used on a temporary basis

The General Court
The General Court operates at a lower level, dealing with ruling in cases brought by individuals, companies and, in some cases, EU governments. Usually this court

deals, for example, with competition law, State aid, trade, agriculture, and intellectual rights.

The constitution of the General Court comprises:
- A President,
- Head of Private Office,
- Vice President,
- 8 Readers of Judgement,
- 9 Presidents of the Chamber
- 47 Judges (increases to 56 in 2019, two judges for each member country),
- 138 Legal Secretaries
- Registrar,
- Deputy Registrar
- Head of Unit B.

Departments of the Court
As stated, the administrative needs of the courts are dealt with by the Departments of the Court. This comprises two main Directorates, the Directorate of the Court and the Directorate General for Administration. Without going into detail on employees the general breakdown of these units is as follows.

Directorate of the Court
- Research and Documentation (3 Units, each with a Head of Unit),
- Protocol and Visits (1 Unit with Head),
- Legal Adviser for Administrative cases (Director),
- Internal Auditor (Director),

- Terminology Projects and Co-ordination Unit (Head of Unit).

Directorate General for Administration
- Directorate for Human Resources and Personnel Administration (4 Units, each with Head of Unit),
- Directorate for Budget and Financial Affairs (2 Units, each with head of Unit),
- Building Directorate (3 Units, each with head of Unit),
- Logistics Directorate (3 Units, each with Head of Unit).

The breakdown, above, does not represent the total staff number. The private offices will be staffed and many of the lower staff levels are not listed. The EU website states that the Court of Justice has 2,174 posts at the end of 2017, but, like other institutions they make use of temporary and occasional staff. When case loading is high extra Advocates may be called upon. Because of the nature of the international work the services of translators are frequently needed and, for example, the Judges and Advocate General have a chauffeur driven car at their disposal, requiring drivers.

Judges at Court of Justice enjoy some of the highest salaries in the EU institutions. As at 2017 the Judges receive a basic salary close to €256,000 per year.

There are extras in the form of allowances and, with these a judge can earn more than €300,000 a year.

Household allowance and one child allowance can be worth up to €9,500. Each judge is entitled to a car and chauffeur.

When appointed, judges receive a once-off installation payment worth two months basic salary, currently €41,664, along with travel expenses for themselves and their family, and furniture-moving costs. The EU feels that when a judge finishes working for the court, to prevent a conflict of interest when seeking further employment, he or she is entitled to a transitional allowance for three years of between €100,000 and €162,493. A judge may also retain the family allowance for that period and receive a once-off resettlement allowance of €20,832.

Judges are entitled to a pension at 65 years of age. Based on final salary and depending on service, it cannot exceed 70 per cent of basic salary, or €174,993 a year. A pension may be drawn from aged 60 at a lower rate.

The highest paid EU judges are the President and the Vice-President. Their basic salary is 138 per cent and 125 per cent of the top civil service rate, which equates to more than €314,000 and €284,400 respectively. They are also entitled to higher entertainment allowances – more than €1,400 and month and €900 a month respectively.

THE EUROPEAN CENTRAL BANK

The European Central Bank (ECB) conducts the monetary policy for the EU and its stated main mission is to maintain price stability and safeguard the Euro. To do this the ECB:

- Supervises credit institutions located in the EU,
- Contributes to the safety and soundness of the banking system and stability of the financial system within the EU.

These aims seem to be relatively simply stated, but when the organisation of the ECB is examined the achievement of those objectives must be much more complicated to require such a large organisation. The EU website states that the ECB employs over 2,500 staff.

The main function of the ECB is to fulfil the aims stated above but it does perform some of the functions of a bank in that it will lend to banks, within the Eurozone. This normally takes the form of short term loans, for example overnight, in order to achieve stability of the currency.

The ECB is the central core of a layered banking system and joins with the Central Banks of all member countries to give two more entities. These are the **European System of Central Banks (ESCB)** and the **Eurosystem.**

- **The ESCB** – comprises the ECB and the National Central Banks of all member countries.
- **The Eurosystem** – comprises the ECB and the National Central Banks of those countries that have adopted the Euro currency.

The organisation of the ECB comprises the following:
- **a Governing Council (including an Executive Board)**
- **a General Council.**

Governing Council

The governing council is the main decision making body of the ECB. The Executive Board functions to provide the day-to-day running of the ECB. It meets twice monthly and comprises:
- A six member **Executive Board**, comprising:
  - a President
  - a Vice President
  - 4 Executive Members.
- Governors of the 19 Eurozone member national banks.

General Council of the ECB

The General Council, primarily, provides an advisory and coordinating role in support of the ECB activity. It comprises the:
- President of the ECB,
- Vice President of the ECB
- Governors of the National Banks of all EU member states.

Supervisory Board

The Supervisory Board meets twice a month to discuss, plan and carry out the ECB's supervisory tasks. It proposes draft decisions to the Governing Council under the non-objection procedure.

The EU website stated composition of the Supervisory Board comprises:
- a Chairperson,
- a Vice person,
- 1 ECB representative
- 5 representatives of the National Supervisors.

However, a photograph on the same web page has a photograph which purports to be the full board composition and shows 30 members. Presumably the additional persons are from the departments listed below.

The Supervisory Board operates with 4 departments and a Secretariat. The departments have the titles:
- Micro-Prudential Supervision I
- Micro-Prudential Supervision II
- Micro-Prudential Supervision III
- Micro-Prudential Supervision IV

As the titles suggest a primary activity of the board is to carry out supervisory activity of all the banks, which includes on-site inspection and audit. They also operate in risk analysis and crisis management.

Administration and Directorates
Providing support and administration for the ECB are:
- 22 Directorates General,
- 5 Directorates,
- a Counsel to the Executive board
- a European Risk Board Secretariat,

- an ECB representative in Washington DC (USA)
- an ECB representative in Brussels (The ECB is located in Frankfurt).

The 22 Directorates General are too numerous to list fully. The EU website, when consulted on ECB managers, has an 8 page listing for managers in banking supervision and a 10 page listing for other managers.

In the employments section for the ECB a currently listed post of Head of Division – Senior Adviser shows a monthly "Net" salary of €7,694. Additionally the ECB will pay 20.7334% of that salary figure into its pension fund. They also provide two thirds payment of health and accident insurance for the permanent employee. Tax will be paid to the EU, which enjoys a lower rate of tax than many national systems.

For the same post, on a short term contract, the Net salary is quoted as €8,704 per month.

THE EUROPEAN COURT OF AUDITORS

The European Court of Auditors (ECA) is the EU institution for auditing the EU's finances. It was not established until 1977 and only became an EU institution in 1993. This says something about the growth of EU spending and the need to keep a check on that spending. It has been described, perhaps with good reason, as the EU's "Financial Watchdog".

The stated objectives of the ECA are to:
- Improve EU financial management,
- Promote accountability and transparency,,
- Act as the independent guardian of the financial interests of the citizens of the EU,

The ECA comprises a collegiate body of 28 members, one from each member country. A president is chosen form one of those members. The organisational structure is as follows:
- **President,** who has**:**
  - Principal manager – Legal Matters
  - Principal manager - Data Protection
  - Principal manager – Internal Auditor.

- **5 Chambers**:
  - Chamber I – Sustainable use of Natural Resources
  - Chamber II – Investment for Cohesion, Growth and Inclusion
  - Chamber III – External Action, Security and Justice
  - Chamber IV – Regulation of the Markets and Competitive Economy
  - Chamber V – Financing and Administering the Union.

  Each chamber is headed by a Dean who controls 4 or 5 members in each chamber. Each Chamber administration requires a Director and 5 Principal Managers. The members each have a private office administered by a Head of Private Office, assisted by an Attaché.

- **Audit Quality Control Committee**
  The EU website shows the makeup of this committee as comprising six members, but, one of these members is a Dean from one of the Chambers above. However, the Dean does not appear to head the Committee, this role appears to be given to a member.

  The Committee is administered by a Director and two Principal Managers. Additionally each member has an office which is administered by a Head of Private Office and an Attaché.

- **Administrative Committee**
  The Administrative Committee comprises the 5 Deans from the chambers, above, and 2 Members. The members have the same office arrangements as other members.

Secretariat General to the ECA

The Secretariat General of the ECA comprises:
- A Secretary general, with a Head of Private Office and an Attaché
- 3 Directors:
  - Director Human Resources, Finance and General Services, with 3 Principal managers
  - Director Information, with 3 Principal Managers

o Director Translation Language Services,
     which has 4 Coordination departments
     and 23 language Teams.

The quoted staffing levels of the ECA are taken from
their website which gives a number of "around 900 staff
in audit, translation and administration". The Salary
table gives a figure for the Member grade as €21,472 per
month (note per month) without allowances. Allowances
will vary according to the circumstances of the
individual.

THE EUROPEAN EXTERNAL ACTION SERVICE

The European External Action Service (EEAS) forms
the Diplomatic Service, Foreign Ministry and Defence
Ministry of the EU. Prior to 2010 The Commission and
the Council of the EU each had an External Relations
Department. In a rare case of what appears to be
rationalisation and economy it was decided to merge the
two external relations department into one entity, named
as the EEAS. However, what has happened since seems
to have been the creation of an ever expanding
organisation that is set upon infiltrating the world.
(Please go to the website "eeas.europa.eu" and find the
Organisation Chart). There you will see a bewildering
display of titles, acronyms and functions, and remember
this will not be all. For every box there will be
supporting functionaries. The annual budget, for 2015,
of the EEAS was €976.1 million.

The EEAS began as an independent institution of the EU in 2011. Its head enjoys the title of "High Representative for Foreign Affairs and Security Policy". Additionally the High Representative is also the President of the Foreign Affairs Council and a Vice President of the Commission. In EU jargon this post is normally shown as HR/VP.

EEAS Organisation
The organisation chart, mentioned above, indicates just how large the organisational layers are. To give some dimension to this huge entity the office of the HR/VP is detailed, followed by the senor management positions.

HR/VP Office
The HR/VP office has a cabinet that comprises the following;
- HR/VP
  o Personal Assistant to the HR/VP
  o 2 Assistants to the HR/VP
  o Logistics Assistant to the HR/VP
- Head of Cabinet
  o Assistant
- Deputy Head of Cabinet
  o Assistant
- Economic Advisor
- 7 Members
  o 5 Assistants to Members
- Expert – Sub-Saharan Africa
- 2 Archivists
- EEAS Spokesperson

- 6 Press Officers
- 2 Press Assistants.

Senior Management positions
In the organisational chart, and listing of the EEAS managerial positions, the following posts are given:
- Secretary General
  - 3 Deputy Secretary Generals

- 2 Director General
  - Deputy Director General
- 6 Managing Director
  - 3 Deputy Managing Directors
- 15 Directors
- 4 Directors/Deputy managing Directors

Activities of the EEAS
The roles given for the EEAS are stated as:
- Manages the EU's diplomatic relations with other countries
- Conducts EU foreign and security policy.

Diplomatic Services
One of the stated activities of the EEAS is stated as the Diplomatic Service. To begin with the EEAS instituted "Delegations" in a number of countries throughout the world. More recently many of these delegations have become "Embassies". Each embassy has an EU ambassador and they operate in a similar way to the national embassies of countries, except that they

promote the wider interests of the EU over the narrower national interest. Currently there are 143 such embassies, or delegation offices, spread across the world.

Foreign and Security Policy
Included in the areas of foreign and security policy are quoted, peace building, security, maintaining good relations, development and humanitarian aid, tackling climate change, and human rights issues. Currently the EEAS website indicates there are 17 Military and Civilian missions and operations, in various parts of the world. Also, so far in 2018, the EU has mounted 8 Election Observation Missions in other countries.

The EEAS has a military element, EU Military Staff (EUMS) headed by a Director General, who will be a senior military figure from one of the member states.

An offshoot of the EEAS is the EU Intelligence and Situation Centre, which is described as an intelligence body of the EEAS. Under a Director it employs 110 people who are engaged gathering and analysing information. The centre is also involved in crisis management and response.

The EEAS website has a Human Resources report, dated for 2015, which states that it employs 4,189 staff. A more recent figure has been given a 4,995 staff, but this is not from the EEAS source. Given the rate at which this institution seems to be growing, the later figure is plausible. The EEAS website also states that 3,616

Commission staff are deployed to delegations throughout the world to assist the EEAS personnel.

COMMITTEE OF THE REGIONS (CoR)

The European Committee of the Regions is a consultative assembly of regional and local representatives that can make an input to the EU institutions. It represents the regions at provincial, county municipality and city levels. It was established in 1994 to give local and regional representatives a say in the development of EU laws. EU treaties oblige the EU Commission and the Council to consult the CoR when proposals are made that may have an impact at the regional; or local level. The CoR can also draw up opinions which it can then submit to the EU institutions, including the right to approach the European Court of Justice.

The CoR has 350 Full members and 350 Alternate Members who are regionally and locally elected and include regional presidents, mayors and councillors. The CoR is headed by a President, supported by a First Vice President

Members of the CoR usually meet six times per year for discussion and to adopt opinions, reports and resolutions. Six Commissions operate to structure the work in specialised areas.

Organisation
- **Presidency**
  - President
  - First Vice President

The Presidency has a Cabinet comprising a Head of Cabinet and 6 Administrators

- **Bureau**
  - 27 Vice Presidents
  - Presidents of the six Political Groups of the EU
  - 32 Members

- **National Delegations**
  - 350 Full Members
  - 350 Alternate Members

- **Commissions**
  - Commission for Natural Resources
  - Commission for Citizenship, Governance. Institutional and External Affairs
  - Commission for Social Policy, Education, Employment, Research and Culture
  - Commission for Economic Policy
  - Environment, Climate Change and Energy
  - Territorial Cohesion Policy and EU Budget

Each Commission has a President, First Vice President and up to 100 Members.

- **Political Groups**
  - Group of the European Peoples Party
  - Party of the European Socialists
  - Alliance of Liberal Democrats
  - European Alliance
  - Conservatives and Reformists
  - Non Attached

Each Political Group, except for the Non Attached Group, is headed by a President and Vice President and has from 8 members (Non Attached) up to over 100 for the larger groups.

Each Political Group, except for the Non Attached, has a Secretariat, headed by a Secretary General, supported by 3 to 9 Administrators.

- **Secretariat General**
  - Secretary General

    Cabinet of the Secretary General
    - Head of cabinet
    - 3 Administrators

    Advisers to the Secretary General
    - Adviser

    Internal Audit
    - Head of Unit
    - Administrator

    Protocol Service
    - Head of Unit

    Directorate A – Members and Plenaries
    - Director

- Deputy Director
- 2 Administrators

Directorate A then has three further units each with a Head of Unit and from 3 to 8 Administrators.

Directorate B – Legislative Work 1

- Director
- Deputy Director
- 3 Administrators

Directorate B then has three further units each with a Head of Unit and from 3 to 8 Administrators.

Directorate C – Legislative Work 2

- Director
- Deputy Director
- 2 Administrators

Directorate C then has three further units each with a Head of Unit and from 3 to 8 Administrators.

Directorate D – Communication

- Director
- Deputy Director
- 2 Administrators

Directorate D then has three further units each with a Head of Unit and from 3 to 8 Administrators.

Directorate E – Human Resources and Finance
- – Director
- – Deputy Director
- – 1 Administrator

Directorate E then has four further units each with a Head of Unit and 3 or 4 Administrators.

The data from 2015 showed that the total number of CoR staff was 527. In the 2018 report the Secretary General states that he heads a staff of over 600. Note that the National Members do not receive a salary from the EU but do receive travel expenses, and its associated allowances, for the attendance at meetings and plenary sessions. The CoR budget for 2013 was €36.5 Million. In 2014 this budget had risen to €90.2 Million and for 2015 the figure was €89.2 Million.

The CoR performs in a similar way to the Economic and Social Committee. The CoR represents at a local level and if the populace is consulted it could be called the instrument of the people's voice. The Economic and Social Committee, which follows, represents organisations.

EUROPEAN ECONOMIC AND SOCIAL COMMITTEE

The EU Economic and Social Committee (EESC) is a grouping of employer organisations, employee organisations and representatives of various bodies throughout the member states of the EU. It is an advisory and consultative body only.

It was originally established to bring together groups that were interested in playing a part in the formation of the Single Market of the EU states. The EESC formed a linking between itself and the Commission and EU Parliament and the people of Europe, thus, allowing their voices to be heard..

Although it has no direct powers, some of the EU treaties stipulate that the EESC must be consulted on specific issues. Additionally institutions can request consultations where it feels the need.

The EESC now declares its role to be consultative and advisory in matters of social policy, social and economic cohesion, environment, education, health, consumer protection, industry, and indirect taxation. In many cases it works together with the Committee of the Regions (CoR).

The structure of the committee is in three equal number groups, employers, employees and third party interests, such as farmers, consumer groups and professional bodies. The EESC membership is currently 350 (which is the same number of members as the CoR). Members are first nominated by their member states and then appointed by the EU Council. After appointment the members agree to be independent of their member states governments.

EESC Organisation.
The organisational structure of the EESC comprises:
- A Presidency
- Bureau of the EESC and Quaestors Group
- A Group Secretariat and specified Groups
- Specialist Sections
- A Consultative Committee on Industrial Change
- A General Secretariat.

Presidency
The Presidency comprises:
- President
  - 2 Vice presidents

The President has a private office which consists of:
- Head of Cabinet
- 4 Administrators
- 5 Assistants

Bureau of the EESC and Quaestor Group
The Bureau of the EESC comprises:
- A President
  - 2 Vice Presidents
  - 33 Members

The Quaestor Group Comprises:
- 3 Quaestors

(Quaestor is a Latin term which originated with the Romans and loosely means an   official. It was first applied to officials who had financial authority).

Specialist Sections

The Specialist Sections of the EECC, with their organisation, are the:

- Single Market Production and Consumption
    - President
    - 2 Vice Presidents
    - 131 Members
- Economic and Monetary Union and Economic and Social Cohesion
    - President
    - 3 Vice Presidents
    - 121 Members
- Employment, Social Affairs and Citizenship
    - President
    - 3 Vice Presidents
    - 130 Members
- Agriculture, Rural Development and the Environment
    - President
    - 3 Vice Presidents
    - 89 Members

- Transport, Energy, Infrastructure and the Information Society
    - President
    - 3 Vice presidents
    - 117 Members

- External Relations
    - President
    - 4 Vice presidents
    - 134 Members

The Consultative Committee on Industrial Change (CCMI).

This Committee succeeded the consultative committee of the European Coal and Steel Community, the forerunner of the EU, which expired in 2002. Its brief is to examine changes in industry across a wide range of sectors to ensure they accord with the values of the European economic and social model

The CCMI works with the Parliament, Council and Commission, giving opinions, or responding to requests from those bodies. It holds conferences and hearings and produces information reports.

The organisation of the CCMI comprises:
- President
  - 50 Delegates
  - 50 Members

General Secretariat

The General Secretariat of the EESC has a Secretary General who has 2 Administrators. It then goes into 9 bodies, listed below. These bodies are then further subdivided into supporting entities, just too numerous to list. If you wish to explore these entities go to europa.eu/whoiswho. There you will find all the institutions listed and you can select the EESC and explore.

The main bodies of the General Secretariat are:
- Internal Audit

- Directorate A – Legislative Planning, Relations with Institutions and Civil Society
- Directorate B – Legislative Works
- Directorate C – Legislative Works
- Department D – Communications
- Directorate E – Human Resources and Finance
- Directorate of Logistics
- Directorate of Translation
- Staff Representative's Secretariat

The directorates will have a Director, with possibly an assistant. Then follow lower level offices, each with a head of unit who oversees, secretaries and assistants etc.

The effectiveness of the EESC and the CoR

The EESC and the CoR have faced a number of calls for their abolition. In 2002 the EU Parliamentary Budget Control Committee called for the EESC to be wound up. But it still exists. Given that the single market was, then, fully in operation the original reason for the CoR was now fulfilled, so, it too has lost its original purpose.

In 2003 the Danish prime minister, and former MEP, stated she believed that these institutions were "too costly and were not giving sufficient value". In response to the recommendation to abolish the two bodies, the Commission included an enhanced role, and budgets, for the two committees, in the Lisbon Treaty.

The CoR claims to provide "Institutional representation for all areas and regions". But, Member states already represent their own regional interests through their governments' participation in the Councils and the MEP's in the parliament. Many of the regions also have a direct representation in Brussels.

In 2011 the Alliance of Liberals and Democrats in Europe issued a draft paper calling for the abolition of both institutions. Following pressure from its members in the CoR the published paper recommended a restructuring instead.

In 2012 the Vice President of the European Conservatives and Reformists Group, of the parliament stated he believed that neither body had been successful in fulfilling its mandate. He also gave some facts on the budgets, stating that over eight years the budgets had doubled to €130 million for the EESC and €86.5 million for the CoR. He further stated that 50 officials in each committee had a minimum salary of €123,890 and six officials in each committee earned over €180,000. Bear in mind these are figures for 2012.

It is estimated that over half of the budgets for these two groups are spent on staff salaries and pensions, and expenses and travel costs. Average travel expenses were estimated at €49,000.

In 2010 the 344 members of the EESC produced 181 opinions, which worked out at an average of €660,000 per opinion. No information is available regarding how these opinions may have influenced any legislation. Again, following the economic crash of 2008 calls were made for the abolition of the EESC, but, it still continues in 2018.

EU DECENTRALISED AGENCIES

The Decentralised agencies are specialist bodies that have been established to provide advice to the EU and the member states. They are located in the member states throughout the EU. The agencies comprise more than 40 bodies. Usually the agency comprises all member states, except that in some cases a state can opt out from an agency. Also non-member states can be included in some agencies where there is a common agreement and interest in the work of that agency. Furthermore a non-member state can be come a cooperating member where there is a common interest. For example the European Environmental Agency includes all EU member states, plus Iceland, Liechtenstein, Norway, Switzerland and Turkey as associate members; Albania, Bosnia Herzegovina, Macedonia, Montenegro and Serbia are cooperating states.

Basic information on the agencies is shown in the following table. The information given is from an EU brochure of 2016, with budgetary information from the 2015 budget.

Agency	Location	Formation	Role	Staff	2015 Budget (million)
Cooperation of Energy Regulators	Slovenia	2011	Telecommunications sector	90	€15.8

Agency	Location	Formation	Role	Staff	2015 Budget (million)
Bio-based Industries Joint Undertaking	Belgium	2014	Development of Sustainable Bio-based Industry	22	€209.4
Translation Centre for EU Bodies	Luxembourg	1994	EU Translation Agency	200	€49
Centre for development of Vocational Training	Greece	1975	Promoting learning for work	119	€18.35
Law Enforcement Training	Hungary	2005	European & Inter-national cooperation training	51	€8.5
Clean Sky 2 Joint Undertaking	Belgium	2008	Research in Aeronautics	42	€351.9
Community Plant Variety Office	France	1995	Innovation & Research by protection of plant Species	45	€15 (but receives fees)
European Aviation Safety Agency	Germany	2002	Aviation Safety	833	€150
Asylum Support Office	Malta	2011	EU Asylum Agency	126	€15.9
European Banking Authority	France (2019) Ex UK	2011	Banking Supervision	151	€33.5
Centre for Disease prevention and control	Sweden	2005	Defence against Infectious Diseases	290	€58.4
European Chemicals Agency	Finland	2007	Chemical Safety	600	€107
European Defence Agency	Belgium	2004	Defence Cooperation	130	€30.5
Environment Agency	Denmark	1994	Environment Improvement	205	€41.7

Agency	Location	Formation	Role	Staff	2015 Budget (million)
Fisheries Control	Spain	2005	Fisheries Control	57	€9.217
Food Safety Authority	Italy	2002	Food Law & Consumer Protection	447	€76.9
Gender Equality	Lithuania	2010	Knowledge Centre on Gender Equality	42	€7.62
Insurance and Occupational Pensions	Germany	2011	Insurance and Pensions	137	€20.6
Innovation & Technology	Hungary	2008	Innovation & Entrepreneurship	59	€295.1
European Medicines Agency	United Kingdom	1995	Evaluation & Super-vision of Medicine	890	€304.1
Centre for Drugs & Drug Addiction	Portugal	1993	Monitoring EU Drugs Problem	100	€15.3
Maritime Safety Agency	Portugal	2002	Safety at Sea $ Cleaner Oceans	207	€54.2
Network & Infor-mation Security	Greece	2004	EU Cyber Security	84	€10.1
Securities and Markets Authority	France	2011	Financial Regulatory Authority	194	€39.392
European Training Foundation	Italy	1994	External Assistance in Human Development	130	€20.1
Institute for Security Studies	France	2002	EU Foreign & Security Policy	24	€5.35
Management of Large Scale IT	Estonia/France	2011	Providing ICT Support	140	€67.1
Safety & Health at Work	Spain	1994	Work Health & Safety	64	€15.2

Agency	Location	Formation	Role	Staff	2015 Budget (million)
Intellectual Property Agency	Spain	1994	Intellectual Property Protection	793	€384.2
Improvement of Living & Working Conditions	Ireland	1975	Social and Work related Research	108	€21
Judicial Cooperation Unit	Netherlands	2002	Justice, Home Affairs & Organised Crime	350	€33.818
Agency for Railways	France	2004	Development of Single European Railways	160	€27.7
European Police Office	Netherlands	1999	EU law Enforcement	1008	€95.4
Fusion and Energy	Spain	2007	Fusion & Energy Development	463	€385.2
Fuel Cells & Hydrogen 2	Belgium	2014	Research into Fuel Cells and Hydrogen	26	€114.615
Agency for Fundamental Rights	Austria	2016	Protection of Fundamental Rights	107	€21.6
Borders & Coast Guard Agency	Poland	2004	Support to EU States	366	€143.3
Global Navigation Satellite Systems	Czech Republic	2004	Linking Space to User needs	140	€27.6
Innovative Medicines	Belgium	2008	Health Research & Drug Development	47	€315.2
European Satellite Centre	Spain	2002	Exploiting Space Assets	120	€17.9
Single European Sky	Belgium	2007	Air Traffic management	41	€89.36
Shift 2 Rail	Belgium	2014	Railway Research &	15	€920

Agency	Location	Format ion	Role	Staff	2015 Budget (million)
			Innovation		
Single Resolution Board	Belgium	2015	Banking Union Resolution Planning	164	€22 (but receives fees)

In two cases the cost to the EU budget is reduced, or zero, because the agency in question receives a fee for its work, or the agency is subscribed by the European banking members.

It is significant to note that until 2002 there were only 11 decentralised agencies, but since that time the number has increased to 44. The politicisation that followed the Lisbon treaty brought about a massive increase in the EU political activities. It has been suggested that some of the agencies are duplicating the work of national agencies and the effectiveness of the activity is in doubt.

The published document, from which this table is produced, is dated at 2016 and it is likely that the staff numbers do not reflect the current levels. For example the Shift 2 Rail agency number in the table is 15 but a recent photo from the agency website shows 18 staff. Given that this agency has a budget of 920 million Euros it is likely that further increase is likely.

EXECUTIVE AGENCIES

Executive agencies are created by the Commission for specific purposes and are set to operate for a fixed term.

These agencies are "third party" bodies and are charged with the implementation of specific EU spending programmes. The Executive agencies are outlined in the following.

Consumers, Health, Agriculture and Food Executive Agency

This agency manages programmes for the EU in support of:

- Consumers
- Public Health
- Agriculture and Rural Development
- Food safety training

The agency was established in 2014, in Luxembourg, and is a third reincarnation. In 2005 the Executive Agency for the Public Health Programme (PHEA) was formed by the EU Commission and lasted until 2008. Then the PHEA became the Executive Agency for Health and Consumers. Finally in 2014 it took its current title.

The 2018 annual work programme for this agency showed that it had 71 staff members, headed by a director. The operating budget for that year showed at 10.566 million Euros. The report also showed that the activities are not just confined to the EU. The following is an extract from the report

> "With respect to organisation of events and campaigns in third countries, up to two high level missions (one will take place in China in May 2018) will be organised during 2018. Communication campaigns will be launched namely in Canada, Middle East, China and Japan. These campaigns

will include organisation of various communication activities, among which participation in international fairs and organisation of promotion seminars. As a follow up of the high level mission to Iran and Saudi Arabia, promotion seminars and/or study visits may be organised in these countries."

Education, Audiovisual and Cultural Executive Agency

This agency manages a number of EU funding programmes on behalf of Commission departments. The major programmes are:

- Creative Europe – Culture and Audiovisual media
- Erasmus – Education, Training Youth and Sport
- Europe for Citizens – Remembrance and Civic Partnership
- EU Aid Volunteers – Training of volunteers and humanitarian organisation
- Intra-Africa Mobility Scheme – Academic mobility in Africa

There are number of lesser projects that arise from funding programmes selected from 2007 to 2013 calendars. For more detail visit the agency website.

The purpose of the agency is best shown by the mission statement form the agencies 2017 annual work report.

"Our mission is to support European projects that connect people and cultures, reach out to the world and make a difference. Working together in education, culture, audio-visual, sport, youth, citizenship and humanitarian aid, we foster innovation through the exchange of knowledge, ideas and skills in a spirit of cross-border cooperation and mutual respect. We strive to provide excellent programme management and high quality service through transparent and objective procedures, showing Europe at its best."

The same report shows that the agency is headed by a Director, supported by a Head of Department who, together, oversee 13 Units. The staff number was shown as 442, but 42 of those were financed from external contributions. The operating budget for that year was 50.217 million Euros, but €47.081 million was EU funding and the rest from external contributions.

Executive agencies manage the funding calls from other bodies. The total budget managed by such agencies for 2017 was, typically, 1.753 billion Euros of EU funding.

European Research Council Executive Agency (ERC)
Established by the EU Commission in 2007 The ERC is a body for the funding of scientific and technology research. The ERC was preceded by a number of Framework Programmes FP1 to FP7 which ran from 1984 until 2013. Following this the name was changed to Horizon 2020 in 2014. This programme is scheduled to run until 2020, but some of its work is being managed by the ERC.

The mission statement for the ERC, taken from their 2017 annual statement of work, states:
"The aim of the European Research Council (ERC) is to provide attractive and flexible funding to enable talented and creative individual researchers and their teams to pursue ground-breaking, high-gain/high-risk research in any field at the frontier of science."

The funding budget for the period 2014-2020 has been planned at over €13 billion.

The ERC is headed by a Director, who has an Assistant Director, 2 Secretaries and a Chief Accountant. This administrative group oversee 5 Units.

The operating budget from the 2018 annual report is given at a total 69.58 million Euros. Of which 65.66 is direct EU funding and the remainder from external contributions.

Executive Agency for Small and Medium-sized Enterprises (EASME)

EASME began in 2003 as the Intelligent Energy Executive Agency. It was intended as a temporary agency but was renamed, in 2007 as the European Agency for Competitiveness and Innovation. It became EASME in 2014. From its annual report it stated vision objective is –

> "We aim to help create a more competitive and resource-efficient European economy based on knowledge and innovation."

It manages programmes for the EU in the fields of Energy, Environment and Business Support. Among those managed are:

- Competitiveness of Enterprise and Small and medium-sized Enterprises
- Part of Horizon 2020
- Part of EU programme for Environment and Climate action

- European Maritime and Fisheries Fund
- Legacy of Intelligent Energy-Europe and Eco-innovation

In managing these programmes EASME states "We ensure that actions funded by these programmes deliver results and provide the Commission with valuable input for its policy tasks".

The Agency is managed by a Director with an Assistant, a Senior Coordinator and a Senior Adviser. They oversee 3 Departments which are divided into 8 Units and 38 Sectors.

In the 2018 Annual report the new Director proclaims he has "close to 500 staff" and has an operational budget of 43.7 million Euros. The EU funding for projects and some external contributions enable him to administer a total budget of 1.3 Billion Euros.

Innovation and Network Executive Agency (INEA)
The Trans European Network Executive agency was formed by the Commission in 2006 to instigate the TEN-T programme (Trans-European Transport Networks). This agency ceased activity at the end of 2013 and Became INEA in 2014. The principal objective is to increase the efficiency of the technical and financial management of its programmes.

INEA is charged with managing the following projects:
- Connecting Europe facility
- Parts of Horizon 2020

- Legacy programmes of the TEN-T and Marco Polo projects

These projects represent all modes of transport – air, road, rail and sea. Also included is Intelligent Transport Systems.

From the INEA annual work report for 2017 the organisation is shown as having a Director, with an Assistant and an Accountant. These manage 3 Departments which are sub-divided into 12 Units.

The 2017 budget was €24.972 million. The staff number was given as 272, with 5 of those being financed from external sources.

Research Executive Agency
REA began operating in 2009 with the states objective "to assist the Commission in achieving the objectives of the Research Framework Programmes and the strategies to foster growth through research and innovation".The initial budget for the 7th Research Framework Programme for 2007-2013 was €6.4 billion. When the programme changed to Horizon 2020 the REA budget for the period 2014-2020 was revised to €17 billion. The annual work report for 2017 showed an operating budget of €65.48 million, of which €62.63 million was EU finding and the rest from external contributions. Staff numbers were 697, with 27 of those being financed from external sources. In the 2018 report the budget numbers had risen to €69.575 million, with the EU contribution at €64.590 million.

The Agency is responsible for:
- Managing parts of the Horizon 2020 programme
- Managing parts of the 7th Framework programme
- Handling the contracting and payment of evaluator experts
- Managing the central evaluation facility for Commission Directorates General
- Performing financial viability checks on organisations which receive EU funding
- Managing the Commission Research Enquiry Service

Euroatom Supply Agency (ESA)
The EU Euroatom Treaty created a common nuclear market in the EU. The supply agency was set up to ensure a regular supply of nuclear fuel to users in the EU. It focuses on giving equal access to ores and nuclear fuel and improving the security of the supply process. To prevent dependence on any single supply source it recommends long term contracts that diversify the sources.

The ESA is mainly financed by the EU Commission the bulk of its administrative expenses for salaries, premises, training and IT infrastructure is covered by the Commission budget. It does receive a small financial contribution for expenses, and for 2017 this was €123,000.

Organisation

When compared to the other agencies the ESA organisation seems remarkable, given the nature of its role in the nuclear material supply field. The organisation chart for this agency, based in Luxembourg, shows:

- Director general:
    - Adviser
    - IT Service Manager

1 Unit – Nuclear Fuel Market Operations
    - Head of Unit + Administrative Assistant
        - 2 Sectors – Contract Management Sector (Sector Head + 4 staff) Observatory Sector (Sector Head + 3 staff)

European Joint Undertaking for ITER and the development of Fusion Energy
(ITER – International Thermonuclear Experimental Reactor).

The ITER Organization is an intergovernmental organization that was established by an international agreement signed in 2006. The parties to the ITER agreement are the People's Republic of China; the European Atomic Energy Community (Euratom); the Republic of India; Japan; the Republic of Korea; the Russian Federation; and the United States of America. The project is an international collaboration to demonstrate the scientific and technological feasibility of fusion energy for peaceful purposes. The EU body that is responsible for the EU's contribution to ITER is Fusion for Energy (F4E).

The F4E seat is located in Spain but has other sites in France and Germany. The European Union is the host for the ITER project. Its contribution amounts to 45%, while the other six parties have an in-kind contribution of approximately 9% each.

Fusion is the process which powers the sun, producing energy by fusing together light atoms such as hydrogen at extremely high pressures and temperatures. The benefits of fusion energy are that it is an inherently safe process and it does not create greenhouse gases or long-lasting radioactive waste.

Currently approximately 800 directly employed staff and 500 external contractors work for the ITER Project in France. On a 42-hectare site, in the south of France, building has been underway since 2010. ITER's first Plasma is scheduled for December 2025.

The budgetary requirements for a programme that is experimental are, understandably, complex but the management seems questionable if the events of 2012 are a guide. The budget for that year for ITER had been approved at €100 million. It was then announced that the programme needed another €1.3 Billion by 2013. A tripartite meeting of the Commission, the Parliament and the Council discussed and approved the extra budget.

For a fuller understanding of the programme go to the ITER website at Europa.eu.

European Institute of Innovation and Technology (EIT)

EIT is an independent EU body, located in Hungary and created in 2008. EIT was born from what were seen as failings in the Lisbon Strategy, an initiative of 2000 to deal with the low productivity and stagnation of economic growth in the EU.

The EIT, from its website gives as it vision:

> "is to become the leading European initiative that empowers innovators and entrepreneurs to develop world-class solutions to societal challenged and create growth and skilled jobs"

The EIT mission is to:

> Contribute to the competitiveness of Europe, its sustainable economic growth and job creation by promoting and strengthening synergies and cooperation among businesses, education institutions and research organisations.
>
> Create favourable environments for creative thought, to enable world-class innovation and entrepreneurship to thrive in Europe.

The EU Commission held a public consultation, taking into account more than 700 contributions from experts and the general public before making a proposal for the EIT governance structure to be a two level structure that combines a bottom-up and top-down approach. The budget provided for the period 2014 – 2020 was €2.4 Billion.

In addition to its headquarters EIT has established at least 41 Innovation Communities across EU and non-EU (Swizerland) locations.

The EIT organisation comprises:
- 12 member Governing Board
  - Executive Committee
  - EU Commission Observer

- Director with Accounting Officer and Internal Auditor
  - Chief Operating Officer overseeing 4 Units and 9 Sectors.

PROPOSED AGENCY

In the first half of 2019 the EU proposes to establish another agency, The European Public Prosecutors Office, based in Luxembourg. Not all member states have agreed to participate, Currently 22 states have agreed to cooperate, with the other states deferring a decision to join.

The role of the EPPO will be to investigate and prosecute fraud against the EU budget and other crimes against the EU's financial interests. This will include fraud concerning EU funds of over €10,000 and cross-border VAT fraud cases involving damages above €10 million. Previously only national authorities could investigate and prosecute these crimes and could not act beyond their borders.

Although the main office will be in Luxembourg, delegated Prosecutors will be located in each Member State. The central office will have a European Chief Prosecutor supported by 20 European Prosecutors supported by technical and investigatory staff.

EU INTERINSTITUTIONAL BODIES

The Interinstitutional Bodies operate to provide services across the EU Institutions, Bodies and Agencies. Currently these listed inter-institutional bodies are the:

- Computer Emergency Response Team (CERT-EU)
- European School of Administration
- European Personnel Selection Office
- Publications Office

Computer Emergency Response Team (CERT-EU)
The function of CERT-EU is to assist in the threat management of computer systems for all EU institutions. It supports the IT teams embedded in those institutions and cooperates with other CERT teams in EU countries.

The acronym CERT has been in use for many years and applies worldwide. Therefore, a –EU is added to reference this body specifically to the EU.

As a separate body CERT-EU only became fully operational in 2012. There is very little information available for this body. A short paper on its set-up indicated there was an Acting Head of Unit, with a Deputy and 30 staff members. A later report stated that it was moving to a larger building in Brussels to cater for an expansion of its activities.

European School of Administration
The School of Administration was set up in 2005 to provide training in specific areas for EU staff. Its stated purpose is to help spread common values, promote a better understanding among EU staff and to achieve economies of scale. The school is part of the EU institutions and the staff members are part of the European Civil Service. Its main school is in Brussels with a small unit in Luxembourg.

Activities include Induction Training for new staff, Workplace Basic Skills, Management and Leadership and Wellbeing.

The School organisation chart appears to differ slightly from the whoiswho site. The organisation appears to show as follows:
- Acting Head of Unit
- Deputy Head of Unit
- Secretary
- Information and Communications Assistant

The school than has two entities which are Planning and Organisation and Course Design and Development. The organisation of these follows.

Planning and Organisation
- 2 Administrative Assistants
- 6 Human Resource management (HRM) Assistants – Training Coordinators
- 2 Planning and Programming Assistants
- Financial Assistant
- 2 Administrative Agents
- Logistics Support Coordinator
- Budget Senior Assistant

Course Design and Development
- 4 HRM Officers – Learning Development Adviser and Trainer
- HRM Assistant – Training Coordinator

European Personnel Selection Office (EPSO)

In the earlier days of the EU the separate institutions organised their own recruitment procedure. In 2003 EPSO became operational across the EU to standardise procedures and thus make savings. The current annual budget for EPSO is €21 million, which is calculated to be a saving of 11% against the individual institutions previous operations.

EPSO sets competitive examinations for the recruitment of staff to work across all the EU bodies. Currently EPSO processes an average 70,000 applications a year for around 1,500 places. Testing is carried out in 24 languages.

Currently no information is provided on the EPSO website regarding its staffing or budget costs.

Publications Office of the EU

The Publications Office is tasked with providing all EU publications. These are provided on paper and in the digital format.

The Publications Office has a number of websites that are available. These are:
- EU Bookshop (online library and bookshop of publications from institutions and EU bodies)
- EUR-Lex (gives access to European Law in 24 languages)
- EU Open Data Portal (access to data form EU institutionsand bodies
- EU WhoisWho (Official Directory of the EU. Lists institutions and bodies)
- CORDIS – Community Research and Development Information Service (gives information on all EU funded projects)
- TED – Tenders Electronic daily (information on public procurement. Around 1,700 procurement notices published daily)

The Publications Office has 4 Directorates:
- Directorate A – Information Management
- Directorate B - Production of Publications
- Directorate C – Access to Public Information
- Directorate D – Corporate Services.

Staffing for these Directorates is as follows.

Directorate A – Information Management
- Director
- Administrative Assistant

Then Directorate A has 4 Units:
- **Unit 1. Standardisation**
  - Head of Unit
  - Deputy head of Unit
  - Information and Communications Officer
  - Secretary to Head of Unit
  - 3 Publications Production Assistants
  - Team leader
  - Information and Communications Agent

- **Unit 2. Common Data Repository**
  - Head of Unit
  - Administrative Assistant

  The Common Data Repository has 3 Sectors:

  ### 001 – Monitoring and Validation
  - Head of Sector

- Document Management Officer
- 8 Document Management Assistants

002 – Reception Systems
- Head of Sector
- 2 project Coordinators
- IT Service Officer
- Information Systems Assistant

003 – Repository
- Head of Sector
- 2 IT Service Officers
- Administrative Assistant

- **Unit 3. Information Systems**
  - Head of Unit
  - Deputy Head of Unit
  - Administrative Assistant

Information Systems then has 5 Sectors:
001 – Cloud Systems
- Head of Sector
- IT Projects manager
- 3 IT Project Assistants

002 – Legal Production and Support Systems
- Head of Sector
- 2 IT Project managers

- IT Project Assistant

003 – General Publications and Standalone Systems
- Head of Sector
- IT projects manager
- IT Project Assistant

004 – Collaboration DIGIT and Outsourcing
- Head of Sector
- 3 IT Service Assistants

005 – Resource Management Quality and Testing
- Head of Sector
- IT Service Assistant
- 2 Financial Assistants

- **Unit 4 – Preservation and Legal Deposit**
  - Head of Unit
  - Administration Assistant

Preservation and Legal Deposit has 2 Sectors:
001 – Metadata Enrichment and Identification
- Head of Sector
- 2 Project managers
- 6 Librarians
- Team Leader Senior Assistant

- o £ Information and Communications Assistants

002 – Longterm Preservation
- o Head of Sector
- o Team Leader Senior Assistant
- o Proof Reader
- o 3 Documentalists
- o Archivist
- o 3 Archivist Agents

Directorate B- Production of Publications
- Director
- Secretary to Director
- Administrative Assistant

Directorate B has 4 Units:
- **Unit 1.- Official Journal and Case Law**
  - o Head of Unit
  - o Deputy Head of Unit

Official Journal and Case Law has 4 Sectors:
001 – Official Journal
- o Head of Sector
- o Team Leader
- o 2 Team Leader Senior Assistant
- o 12 Publications Production Assistants
- o Proof Reader

76

002 – Budget and Interoperability
- o Head of Sector
- o Information Systems Assistant
- o Publications Production Assistant
- o Team Leader Senior Assistant

003 – Case Law and Manuscript
- o Head of Sector
- o Team Leader
- o Publications Production Assistant
- o 2 Publications Agents
- o 2 Document Managers

004 – Production Support
- o Head of Sector
- o Policy Senior Assistant
- o 4 Information Assistants
- o Programme Assistant

- **Unit 2. – Multimedia and Publications**
  - o Head of Unit

Unit 2 has 3 Sectors:
001 – Graphic Design and Prepress
- o Head of Sector
- o Infographiste
- o 4 Website Designers

- o 4 Graphics Designers

002 – Publications Projects
- o Head of Sector
- o 19 Website Designers
- o Production Manager

003 – Digital and Mobile Publications
- o Head of Sector
- o Team Leader
- o Information and Communications Officer
- o 3 Publications Production Assistants
- o 4 Website Designers
- o Webmaster, Editor

- **Unit 3 Content and Demand management**
  - o Head of Unit
  - o Deputy Head of Unit

Unit 3 has 3 Sectors:
001 – Publications Domain Leadership
- o Head of Sector
- o 2 Information and Communications Officers
- o Information and Communications Assistants

002 – Demand Management and Planning

- o Head of Sector
- o 12 Information and Communications Assistants

003 – Systems and Tools
- o Head of Sector
- o Information Systems Officer
- o 4 Information Systems Assistants

- **Unit 4 – Quality Control**
  - o Head of Unit
  - o Deputy head of Unit

Quality Control has 3 Sectors:
001 – Quality Control A
- o Head of Sector
- o 32 Proof Readers

002 – Quality Control B
- o Head of Sector
- o Team Leader, Senior Assistant
- o 31 Proof Readers

003 – Quality Control C
- o Head of Sector
- o 31 Proof Readers

Directorate C – Access to and Reuse of Public Information
- Director

- Administrative Assistant

Directorate C has 4 Units:
- **Unit 1 – OP Portal**
  - Head of Unit

OP Portal has 2 Sectors
  001 – Portal Platform and Digital Collaborative Tools
  - Head of Sector
  - 2 Webmaster – Editors
  - 4 Information and Communications Assistants
  - Programme Assistant
  - Senior Assistant
  - Publications Assistant

  002 – OP Collections Action Services
  - Head of Sector
  - Programme Officer
  - Team Leader
  - 2 Information and Communications Assistant
  - IT Service Assistant
  - Administrative Assistant
  - Programme Assistant

- **Unit 2 – EUR-Lex and Legal Information**
  - Head of Unit
  - Deputy Head of Unit

EUR-Lex and Legal Information has 4 Sectors

001 - - EUR–Lex Editorial Content
- Head of Sector
- Legal Officer
- 2 Webmaster – Editors
- Policy Senior Assistant
- 2 Information and Communications Assistants

002 - Support to Dissemination Websites
- Head of Sector
- Project Manager
- 2 Project Assistants

003 – Documentary Management and Legal Analysis
- Head of Sector
- 2 Legal Officers
- Document Management Assistant
- Librarian
- Documentalist
- Proof Reader
- Legal Assistant

004 – Consolidation and Summaries of EU Law
- Head of Sector
- Secretary
- 4 Publications Production Assistants
- 2 Documentalists

- **Unit 3 – TED and EU Public Procurement**
  - ○ Head of Unit
  - ○ Deputy Head of Unit

TED and EU public Procurement has 2 Sectors

001 – Reception, Production and Dissemination
  - ○ Head of Sector
  - ○ Project Manager
  - ○ 2 Webmaster – Editors
  - ○ 2 Administrative Assistants
  - ○ 3 Production Coordinators
  - ○ Administrative Agent

002 – Vision and Support
  - ○ Head of Sector
  - ○ Procurement Business Manager
  - ○ Project Assistant
  - ○ Documentalist

- **Unit 4 – EU Open Data and CORDIS**
  - ○ Head of Unit
  - ○ Deputy Head of Unit
  - ○ Administrative Assistant

EU Open Data and CORDIS has £ Sectors:

001 – EU Open Data
  - ○ Head of Sector

- o 2 Knowledge Management Officers
- o 5 Knowledge Management Assistants
- o Project Assistant

002 – CORDIS
- o Head of Sector
- o 2 Project Officers
- o 5 Project Assistants

003 – Service Development
- o Head of Sector
- o 4 project Assistants

Directorate D – Corporate Services
- Director
- Secretary

Directorate D has 4 Units
- **Unit 1 – Stakeholder Relations**
  - o Head of Unit
  - o Deputy Head of Unit
  - o Secretary

Stakeholder Relations has 2 Sectors:
001 – Corporate Procedures and Customer Relations Management
- o Head of Sector
- o Project Leader
- o 9 Administrative Assistants

- o Information and Communications Assistant
- o 2 Administrative Assistants
- o Team Leader

002 – Promotion and Internal Communication
- o Head of Sector
- o 2 Team Leaders
- o 10 Administrative Assistants
- o Information and Communications Assistant

- • **Unit 2 – Contracts and Copyrights**
  - o Head of Sector
  - o Administrative Assistant

Contracts and Copyright has 3 Sectors

001 – Calls for Tender
- o Head of Sector
- o Finance and Contracts Officer
- o 7 Finance and Contracts Assistants
- o Secretary

002 Contracts
- o Legal Administrator
- o 3 Finance and Contracts Assistants
- o Legal Assistant

003 – Copyright and Legal Issues
- o Head of Sector

- o 3 Legal Assistants
- o Policy Senior Assistant
- o Clerk

- **Unit 3 – Finance**
  - o Head of Unit
  - o Financial Secretary

Finance has 4 Sectors:

001 – Financial Planning and Accounts
- o Head of Sector
- o Senior Assistant
- o 3 Financial Assistants

002 – Financial Implementations and Support
- o Head of Sector
- o 3 Financial Assistants
- o IT Project Officer
- o Archivist

003 – Budget Cell – Official Journal and Information Technology
- o Team Leader
- o 9 Financial Assistants

004 – Budget Cell – General Publications and Resources
- o Head of Sector
- o 11 Financial Assistants

- **Unit 4 – Print and Distribution**
  - o Head of Unit
  - o Deputy Head of Unit
  - o Health and Safety Assistant
  - o Information and Communications Assistant
  - o

Print and Distribution has 2 Sectors:

001- Print
  - o Head of Sector
  - o Team Leader – Senior Assistant
  - o 3 Logistical Support Coordinators
  - o Document Manager
  - o 2 Document Management Agents
  - o Information and Communication Agent
  - o 3 Web Designers

002 – Distribution
  - o Head of Sector
  - o 3 Publications Production Assistants
  - o IT Services Assistant
  - o 3 Administration Assistants
  - o 2 Information and Communication Agents.

This vast organisation exists to produce documents for the bodies of the EU, which it does in enormous

86

quantity. Most of these documents are held digitally or in libraries and the public can access them. But, do you know anybody who has accessed or acquired an EU report?

EU AMBASSADORS

The European Coal and Steel Community opened its first mission, in London, in 1955. Following the merger of the three of three executive institutions of the European Community into the single Commission, in early 1960, the number of delegations increased. At that time the Maastricht Treaty required the diplomatic missions of member states and the EU Delegations to "co-operate in ensuring that the common positions and joint actions adopted by the Council are complied with and implemented"

In 1972 a significant change occurred when the US Congress recognised the EU delegation as having full embassy status and the delegation head was accorded with the rank and courtesy title of Ambassador.

In 1975 the Lomé Convention was signed in Togo. This was a trade and aid agreement between the EEC and 71 African, Caribbean, and Pacific countries. In three years the number of missions in these countries doubled to 41 and the missions were upgraded to full delegations. For the first time diplomatic immunity was given to the heads of the delegations.

By 1980 over 1,000 staff were working in 50 delegations spread throughout the world. Some of these delegations represent a number of countries. A 2013 report showed that the EU is represented in 11 Pacific Island countries, four overseas territories by the delegation in Fiji. The delegation is credited to Cook Islands, Kiribati, Nauru, Niue, Palau, Marshall Islands, Tonga, French Polynesia, Pitcairn and several other territories. There is also a separate delegation in Papua New Guinea with two sub-offices in the Solomon Islands and Vanuatu. (The Vanuatu office was closed in 2013 and the Solomon Islands incorporated Vanuatu).

In 1988 a reform absorbed staff fully into the Commission and the number of Commission delegation staff rose, immediately, from 165 to 440, with a local staff contingent of 1,440. The number of missions had now risen to 89.

By 1990 the most delegations were considered as full diplomatic missions by the host countries, with the delegation head, approved by the Commission, as having the rank and courtesy title of Ambassador.

In 1998 the Amsterdam Treaty created a new post of "High Representative" to the Council and Commission. This effectively set up a second EU foreign service, the previous being the Commissioner for External Relations, for whom the delegations worked.

In 2003 the delegations were now present in over 150 countries, with over 5,000 staff. The delegations are now becoming more political in supporting the campaigns in countries hoping to gain accession to the EU, bearing in mind the original purpose was concerned with trade relations and aid. The political involvement is best illustrated by the 2006 full accreditation to the Vatican and in the following year to the Order of the Knights of Malta, these entities hardly being trading nations, or in need of aid.

In December of 2009 the Treaty of Lisbon created the European External Action Service (EEAS). Its stated intention was to "make the EU's external action more coherent and efficient, thereby increasing the EU's influence in the world. And this it did. Before the Lisbon treaty the EU was represented abroad by the Ambassador of the country that held the EU Presidency and the EU Commission was represented by a Head of Delegation of the European Commission who was given the courtesy title of Ambassador. In 2010, after the Lisbon Treaty, the EU Ambassador was given the title "Ambassador Extraordinary and Plenipotentiary" and was chosen from candidates proposed by the European External Action Service and appointed by the Presidents of the Council and the Commission. As stated, before the treaty, delegations worked with the national diplomatic missions. Now each Head of Delegation was given full ambassadorial status and the staff full diplomatic privileges and immunities. This peculiar arrangement of foreign policy creates a situation for EU member states where they have, effectively two, or three if the Commission is counted, foreign offices; one in the national state and two in Brussels.

Following the creation of the EEAS , by 2013 the EU had embassies in 140 countries and, often, their staffing exceeded that of national embassies. For example Mozambique had 32 personnel, Uruguay 30 and Papua New Guinea 37. This is not surprising since the Lisbon treaty treaties and agreements meant that EU policy was precedent over national policies and the EU embassies were, increasingly taking over from the national embassies. An MEP who was visiting the Lima embassy was quoted as saying:

> "I recently visited the commission's mission to Lima - hardly, you might think, a critical posting. Yet it had a staff of 50, more than any of the 25 national delegations. In part, this reflects the shift in power between the national capitals and Brussels. European embassies in a city like Lima used to be chiefly concerned with trade, aid and visas. The first two of these are now under EU jurisdiction; and although the granting of visas is still up to national consulates, Brussels increasingly decides who qualifies. When I asked the Euro-diplomats what was left for their national counterparts to do, they grinned conspiratorially and muttered something about promoting tourism."

Official figures from EEAS data showed in 2013 that the largest single delegation is based in Ankara, the Turkish capital, and employs a total of 140 people, including staff and "local agents".

EU Ambassadors enjoy the life style of state diplomats. Remuneration is a current salary of €21,300 per month. Added to this are, sickness and pension rights, parental and maternity leave, and €313 monthly child allowance. Taxation is, generally, at a preferential rate and may be as low as 15%. Free accommodation is provided, frequently in luxurious residences that fit the ambassadorial status, First class travel for the whole family, staff cars, or car allowance with mileage allowance are among other perks that go with the role. The EEAS has bought about 650 cars for use by officials in overseas headquarters. The average price of each car is £21,000 although that does not include the much higher extra cost for armoured cars, which are deemed necessary in some locations..

A report from the Open Europe think tank included the statement, "the general problem with the EU's foreign diplomatic service is that it can lead to costly and unnecessary duplication with national governments' embassies, and, political accountability is very weak."

Ambassadors to international organisations
In addition to the Ambassadors to countries the EU also has delegations in some major worlds' organisations. These are:
- African Union – based in Addis Ababa
- Association of Southeast African Nations - based in Jakarta
- Council of Europe - based in Strasbourg
- World Trade Organisation - based in Geneva
- United Nations - based in New York City

- United Nations - based in Geneva
- United Nations - based in Vienna
- Organisation for Security and Cooperation in Europe - based in Vienna
- United Nations Educational, Scientific and Cultural Organisation - based Paris
- Holy See - based in Rome.

Some immediate questions arise from this list. Why does the EU need a delegation to its own institution, the Council of Europe? Why are there three delegations to the United Nations? And the delegation to the Vatican? which, when explored, reveals it is staffed as follows:

- Ambassador - Head of Delegation
- Assistant to the Head of Delegation
- Deputy Minister Counsellor
- Attaché - International Relations, Information & Communication operations
- Administrative Coordination Officer
- Seconded National Expert, Alternate First Secretary
- Junior Professional in Delegation
- Administration Head of Office
- Driver
- 4 Interns

Perhaps the answer to the question "Why the Vatican?" is provided by the Ambassador's introductory message on his website:

"Today, more than ever before, the global aspects of the Holy See's policies are known and followed by many. The increased outreach carried out by the Pope, especially by Pope Francis, has contributed to reaching out to also the general public and not only religious followers. The voice of the Pontiff who addresses the universal question of peace, freedom, dignity of human being, fundamental rights and values triggers the activity of the diplomacy of the Holy See. It reaches billions of people around the world, not exclusively Catholics or Christians. All efforts of the Pope to pave the way for the unity of Christians impact directly on peace perspectives in the world, as well as on the situation within the European continent. The ecumenical dialogue has significant importance for European countries and nations and the interreligious contacts aim at inter alia easing tensions exploited by extremists and radicals.

All these issues are of utmost interest to the European Union and the dialogue aiming at the common action and search for synergies with the Holy See is a part of the Global Strategy of the EU. The Delegation is the first rung interlocutor for the Holy See and for partners who gather behind the Pope and assist His action".

This type of verbose dialogue is common throughout the EU documentation to justify the existence of the spreading number of delegations. Perhaps they should learn from a statement attributed to one of the earlier Popes, who speaking from the opulence of his grand palace is alleged to have stated "This myth of Christ has served us well". I wonder how many EU diplomats could paraphrase this with, "This myth of European Union is serving us well".

EU SPECIAL REPRESENTATIVES (EUSR)

EUSR's are emissaries of the EU who have special roles in areas that have specific issues. The issues may be areas of conflict, security issues or regions that have peculiar geographical features that cause problems. There is also a global position of the EUSR for Human Rights. The EUSR is under the direct control of the High Representative of the EU of Foreign Affairs and Security Policy. The EU Ambassadors may have the dual role as head of delegation or the EUSR may be an individual position, working closely with regional Ambassadors.

Currently there are eight EUSR. They are to:
- Bosnia and Herzegovina
- Central Asia
- Horn of Africa
- Human Rights
- Kosovo
- Middle East Peace Process
- Sahel (The Sahel is an area in Africa between the Sahara in the north and the Sudan Savannah to the south)
- South Caucasus and Georgia

There have also been EU representatives who operate with other world organisations in special areas of interest. For example Tony Blair was the EU envoy to the Middle East from 2007 until May 2015. In this role he also acted for The United Nations, United States and Russia.

OLAF (European Anti-Fraud Office)

In 1998 the Secretariat of the Commission created an "Anti Fraud Coordination Unit. This unit was named in the French language as UCLAF (*Unité de coordination de lutte anti-fraude*). In 1999, as a result of allegations of nepotism and corruption made against a number of Commissioners, the entire Commission resigned. Following criticism of UCLAF, because of its closeness to the Commission, a new body was formed which was given an independent investigative mandate. This body was again named in French as OLAF (*Office européen de lutte antifraude*). The English title is the "European Anti-Fraud Office.

The stated functions of OLAF are to:
- fight fraud affecting the EU budget
- investigate corruption by staff of the EU institutions
- develop anti-fraud legislation and policy

OLAF works with anti-fraud partners in the member states, supporting them with its experience and knowledge. OLAF has no judicial powers to oblige national law enforcement authorities to act on its recommendations. It is still a Directorate General of the

Commission (Budget and Human Resources) but is independent when conducting its investigations.

The 2017 annual report showed that OLAF had a staff of about 420, including police, customs and legal experts from member states. It is headed by a Director General who has 4 Directorates and 20 Units. The budget for 2017 was €60 million.

The report showed the workload for 2017 as:
- following 1,111 preliminary analyses OLAF opened 215 new investigations
- OLAF concluded 197 investigations and issued 309 recommendations
- OLAF recommended the recovery of over €3 Billion as a result of fraud cases.

The absolute effectiveness of OLAF is sometimes questioned. It is still attached to the Commission. OLAF can only issue recommendations, it does not have any powers to prosecute or discipline, only to make recommendations. It is up to the relevant judicial bodies and EU institutions to follow the recommendations and take action or not. Each Member State has their own legal systems, with their own law enforcement and evidence collecting methods and this can make it difficult for OLAF. There is also the problem of cooperation between the state and the agency and at a local level, cultural, legal and language barriers. Many Hungarian authorities have refused to make cooperation agreements with OLAF and, usually do not follow any recommendations. There are reports that the cooperation between OLAF and EUROPOL and EUROJUST is not good because of conflict of jurisdiction issues.

Another criticism levelled against the EU is that its anti-fraud activity is more concerned with keeping improper conduct in-house rather than it being out in the public domain. An example of this is, perhaps, the "Tillack" case, named after a reporter Hans-Martin Tillack.

The Tillack Case

Hans-Martin Tillack was the journalist who, in 2001, brought the public's attention to the EUROSTAT scandal. He published details from a confidential OLAF document revealing the alleged fraud. Two years later, following statements made by a former Commission spokesman, OLAF claimed that Tillack may have received the internal documents from an official in exchange for money. This information was passed to the Belgian public prosecutor. In 2004, following a request from OLAF, a Belgian judge ordered a search of the journalist's home and office in Brussels where the authorities seized his archives and his mobile phone. On the basis of the same information, the German authorities also opened an investigation but decided not to search his German offices.

Tillack initiated legal proceedings in Germany, Belgium, Strasbourg, and before the European Court of Justice. His complaint before the German courts against the Commission spokesman on whose statements OLAF had based the case was unsuccessful, as were his appeals to the Belgian courts. Tillack subsequently took Belgium to the European Court on Human Rights in Strasbourg In 2007 the court condemned Belgium for failing to uphold Article 10 of the European Convention on Human Rights, which enshrines the right of journalists to protect their sources. The court ordered Belgium to pay Tillack costs of €40,000 and compensation of €10,000. The journalist also took OLAF to the European Court of Justice where all his pleas were dismissed. Tillack complained to the European Ombudsman, who wrote a special report in May 2005 in which he recommended that OLAF should acknowledge that it made incorrect and misleading statements in its submissions to the Ombudsman and that the European Parliament could consider adopting his recommendation as a resolution. The European Parliament did not act on the Ombudsman's suggestion.

The 2017 annual report of the OLAF activity gives the details of the major cases investigated, which are too numerous to detail. Limited examples are:

- Risk capital Funds in Germany who made irregular payments in 44 companies that did not meet the eligibility criteria
- Hungary, Latvia and Serbia were involved in sub-contracting schemes that artificially increased project costs
- Italy was involved in a project to develop emergency response Hovercraft. Project funds were diverted to a fictitious company and some of the money was used to pay off a mortgage on a disused castle that was faced with foreclosure.

FRAUD AND CORRUPTION IN THE EU

In an organisation as large and diverse as the EU a measure of fraud is inevitable. In some of the countries the practice of using intermediaries in business negotiations is considered normal, whereas in other countries this is seen as tantamount to paying bribes. High levels of taxation on specific goods such as alcohol and cigarettes make cross border smuggling and tax evasion inevitable. But, a higher level of concern is the fraud and corruption that may be taking place within the institutions and agencies of the EU. Some of these are outlined in the following.

The 1999 Commission Scandal

Following rumours and reports in national newspapers an inquiry was instigated into the allegations of nepotism and mismanagement within the Commission. The report named six individuals who had acted inappropriately and cited a culture of favouritism, complacency, arrogance and mishandling of taxpayer's money. In a damming critique the report argued that the failure of commissioners to keep track of developments was "tantamount to an admission of loss of control". It added that "it was becoming difficult to find anyone who has even the slightest sense of responsibility".

Following the report the whole Commission resigned in March of 1999. The following are the salient points regarding the individual accusations. Full details are available from internet searches.

The president of the Commission, Jacques Santer, was accused of failing to supervise the Commission's security office, for which he was responsible, and which faced allegations of fraud. The report stated "No supervision was exercised and a state within a state was allowed to develop". The president was accused of giving evasive and misleading answers to the European Parliament on Fraud issues. He was cleared on the allegation of favouritism.

The previous president of the Commission, Jacques Delors, was also cited in the report as "failing to follow up allegations of fraud in the Commission's security service".

The Portugese Commissioner, Joao de Deus Pinheiro, appointed his brother-in law as an adviser in his private office. The report concluded that the procedures were correct but further stated "no Commissioner should appoint a close relative to work in his, or her, private office".

The Spanish Vice President of the Commission, Manuel Marin, was criticised for his slow response to fraud within an EU aid project.

A German Commissioner, Monika Wulf-Mathies was criticised for using inappropriate procedures to appoint an associate to her staff.

Edith Cresson, a former French Prime Minister, stood accused of favouritism in appointing a close friend, her dentist, as a scientific adviser. The inquiry stated "his appointment was manifestly irregular, and cited his frequent paid missions to his home town on supposed Commission business as evidence of the "fictitious nature of the scientific advice" he was supposed to be giving. In eighteen months of supposed work he produced only 24 pages of notes, The inquiry further stated that Mrs Cresson also stayed silent in the face of irregularities in the £400m Leonardo project, even though she was "in full possession of the facts". After a gap of 4 years Mrs, Cresson was brought before the European Court of Justice and found guilty of malpractice. She was dismissed from her post with a recommendation that her EU pension should be reduced. This recommendation was not upheld. It was considered that the loss of her job was enough punishment. Presumably, because no financial sanctions were upheld, she was able to leave with a severance payout and, as a Commissioner, she could be allowed to draw up to 65% of her salary for a period of up to 3 years while seeking new employment.

Incredibly the person who instigated the investigations by "whistleblowing" initially received more severe punishment. An official in the Committee on Budgetary Control made a report on perceived irregularity within the Commission. No direct action was taking so the report was leaked. As a result he was suspended from his position, his salary was halved and he was ordered to face disciplinary action. Public interest was aroused by the press and as a result he was reinstated, but, in a different role. His treatment by the Commission was a factor in the resignation of the whole Commission.

The EUROSTAT Scandal

In 2000, internal auditors published concerns about fictitious contracts raised by the European Office for Statistics (EUROSTAT) with outside companies and referred the matter to the European Anti-Fraud Office, (OLAF) who did not take any immediate action. The same official, who acted in the above Commission resignation case, made a second report in 2001. This report was, again not acted upon until the press was made aware and published details. OLAF was now forced into action and produced a report entitled "A vast enterprise for looting Community funds". The report revealed that EUROSTAT used a double accounting system to transfer large amounts of money into secret bank accounts. Between 1996 and 2001 some four to five million Euros was thought to have gone astray.

The report could find no evidence of personal enrichment but three senior officials were removed form their posts and a number of outside contracts were cancelled. Later, in 2008, the Commission was condemned by the European Court of Justice for failures of OLAF and ordered to make payments to two senior Eurostat officials.

The 2006 Galvin Report

An audit of the expenses and allowances of a sample of 160 MEPs was conducted by an official of the EU Internal Audit Office in 2006, Mr. Robert Galvin.

Described as a "shocking report" it was kept secret until 2008 when an MEP revealed its existence. Even then only a select group of MEPs were given access to this report and they were only allowed to see it individually, in a locked and guarded room.

Inevitably the report was leaked and it findings included:
- Serious and repeated anomalies in payments for office assistance and services.
- Dubious large cash payments are made to staff and service providers over and above salaries.
- Improper registration and tax compliance of service providers.
- Invoicing is lax or non-existent.
- Some MEPs are paying set amounts straight into the coffers of their political parties.
- Paying Agents' expense claims are opaque or even unrecorded.

The 2011 Cash for Influence Scandal

A former Austrian MEP was convicted of attempting to change laws in the European Parliament on behalf of a business offering to pay him €100,000 a year. The former minister, who was said to have used his role as an MEP to work secretly as a lobbyist, was exposed during an undercover investigation by the Sunday Times. He was jailed for three years after being found guilty of corruption by a court in Vienna. It was the second time he had been convicted of the same offence. An earlier verdict had been overturned on appeal. The reporters, posing as lobbyists, found two other MEPs who were willing to accept payment for trying to amend legislation.

A Romanian MEP, was also accused of having taken bribes from journalists and charged with siphoning € 436,000 from the EU budget.

EU Budget Fraud
EU budget fraud is a constant problem and ranges from farmers seeking payments for climatically impossible sugar cane cultivation to the payment of funds for immigration projects to, what some have labelled, terrorist groups.

The 2017 annual report of the OLAF activity gives the details of the major cases investigated, which are too numerous to detail. Limited examples are:
- Risk capital Funds in Germany who made irregular payments in 44 companies that did not meet the eligibility criteria
- Hungary, Latvia and Serbia were involved in sub-contracting schemes that artificially increased project costs
- Italy was involved in a project to develop an emergency response Hovercraft. Project. Funds were diverted to a fictitious company and some of the money was used to pay off a mortgage on a disused castle that was faced with foreclosure.

The Luxembourg Leaks Scandal
In 2014 a consortium of Investigative Journalists revealed "confidential" information regarding

Luxembourg's tax laws. The report showed that Luxembourg had approved questionable corporate schemes to avoid tax by major companies. The arrangements put pressure on the Commission president, Jean-Claude Juncker, who was either finance minister, or prime minister of the Grand Duchy when the tax deals were being negotiated. A German MEP has stated that he believes these revelations provide evidence that the Luxembourg state was knowingly complicit in tax evasion on a massive scale.

The investigation showed that beneficial tax rulings for over three hundred multinational companies based in Luxembourg had been given. The European Commission carried out an investigation and brought in new rulings aimed at reducing tax dumping and regulating tax avoidance schemes beneficial to multinational companies.

These are but a few of the cases. An investigation of the OLAF website and their annual reports will show the hundreds of cases investigated each year. A major problem seems to be that follow-up actions on reported cases of fraud or maladministration are few.

THE GROWTH AND EXPANSION OF THE EU

The growth of the EU
A simplified timeline for the evolution of the EU, in terms of growth is:

- 1957 – Treaty of Rome creates the European Economic Community (Common market) with Belgium, France, Germany, Italy, Luxembourg and the Netherlands being founder members.
- 1962 – On becoming independent from France, Algeria exited from the EEC.
- 1973 – Denmark Ireland and UK join. Now 9 members.
- 1979 – Greenland is granted home rule from Denmark and votes to leave the EEC. Finally leaving in 1985 but retaining association through some treaties. 1979 also saw the first direct elections for the EU Parliament.
- 1981 – Greece joins.
- 1986 – Spain and Portugal join.
- 1989 – Following the fall of the Berlin wall East and West Germany are re-united and the German contingent to the EEC increases.
- 1993 – The EEC is incorporated to become the European Community.
- 1995 – Austria, Finland and Sweden join. (Now 15 members)
- 2000 – Common currency, the Euro, is introduced.
- 2004 – 10 new countries join. (Now 25 members)
- 2007 – Bulgaria and Romania join.
- 2009 – Treaty of Lisbon creates the European Union, with more political power.
- 2013 – Croatia joins.

Expansion of the EU

Expansion of the EU, in terms of its structure is shown by the above timeline, but, in terms if political and economic growth the various treaties created the expansion of EU, in terms of growth and influence. These treaties are:

- Establishment of the European Coal and Steel Community (ECSC)

    Came into force in 1952 and expired in 2002. The purpose was to create interdependence in coal and steel so that one country could no longer mobilise its armed forces without others knowing. This eased distrust and tensions after WWII

- Treaty of Rome

    Came into force in 1958 to set up the EEC and the European Atomic Energy Community (Euratom). This extended European integration and economic cooperation.

- Brussels Treaty (Merger Treaty)

    Came into force 1967 with the purpose of streamlining European institutions. It, supposedly, did this by creating a single Commission and a single Council to serve the EEC, Euratom and the ECSC.

- Single European Act

    Came into force in 1987. Its purpose was to reform the institutions in preparation for Portugal and Spain's membership and speed up decision-making in preparation for the single market. The main changes were an extension of qualified majority voting in the Council (making it harder for a single country to veto proposed legislation), and to give the European Parliament more influence by the creation of cooperation and assent procedures.

- Maastricht Treaty (Treaty on European Union)
  In force in 1993. The purpose was to prepare for European Monetary Union and introduce elements of a political union (citizenship, common foreign and internal affairs policy). The significant changes were the establishment of the European Union and introduction of the co-decision procedure, giving Parliament more say in decision-making. Also increased cooperation between EU governments – for example on defence and justice and home affairs

- Treaty of Amsterdam
  In force 1999. The purpose was to reform the EU institutions in preparation for the arrival of future member countries. In this it gave amendment, renumbering and consolidation of EU and EEC treaties. The intention was to create more transparent decision-making and increased use of the ordinary legislative procedure.

- Treaty of Nice
  Came into force in 2003. Its purpose was to reform the institutions so that the EU could function efficiently after reaching 25 member countries. The main changes were to

bring in methods for changing the composition of the Commission and redefining the voting system in the Council.

- Treaty of Lisbon

    Came into force in 2009. The purpose was to make the EU more democratic, more efficient and better able to address global problems, such as climate change. Also it wanted to create an EU with a single voice. The principle changes were to give more power for the European Parliament, to change voting procedures in the Council, to create a permanent president of the European Council, a new High Representative for Foreign Affairs, and a new EU diplomatic service. It also gave rise to the citizens' initiative, wherein if a million signatures can be raised on an issue, it must be considered by the Commission for possible action. It further clarified which powers belong to the EU, belong to the individual member countries or which powers are shared.

In terms of expansion the Treaty of Nice anticipated the addition of 10 more countries and prepared for that growth. The Treaty of Lisbon created the greatest increase in activities. The number of decentralised agencies has increased from just 11 to over 40 from those treaties. The External Action Service was created and has spread its activity throughout the world. Almost every institution and agency has an office concerned with EU enlargement.

Further growth is anticipated. Among the list of candidate countries to join the EU, and add to its enlargement, are - , Serbia, Montenegro, Albania, the Yugoslav Republic of Macedonia and Turkey. Described as "potential" candidates are Bosnia and Herzegovina, and Kosovo.

Nowhere is EU expansion more typified than the European External Action Service. A browse of its website shows that it has 131 Ambassadors in countries or international organisations. It has 143 Delegations throughout the world, and if you query the difference between the roles, the site explains that delegations have the status of diplomatic missions. The chief official of a Delegation is described as Ambassador/Head of Delegation so little difference. Then the site also indicates "Countries" and investigation of this shows the EU has some form of relationship with 206 countries, usually described as a "Partnership Agreement".

A look at one such country that does not show on the Ambassador or the Delegation lists is Timor-Leste, which is half an island in South East Asia; the other half being Indonesian. The EU presence in Timor-Leste is, again, an Ambassador/Head of Delegation who heads a Cooperation Section, a Finance Contracts and Audit Section, and an Admin Section. The Cooperation section has a Head, 7 Programme Officers and a Secretary. The Finance Section currently shows no staff list while the Admin Section has a head, 5 supporting staff and 2 drivers. This is for half an island, with a population of 1.2 million whose main production crop is coffee and has some offshore Oil and Gas reserves. Another interesting fact from the Timor-Leste research concerns the EU Ambassador. He is Portuguese and until the mid 1970's East Timor was colony of Portugal. With the EEAS, are we witnessing a subtle and more benign way of re-colonising?

Investigations like this show that the EU published list of Ambassadors is not the complete list. Delegation heads enjoy Ambassadorial status as do, it appears, the heads of missions to lesser countries. All of these EU officials are in addition to any officials that national governments may have in the locations.

Again, for the conspiracy theorists, if you look closely at the organisation chart for the EEAS, its 126 organisational blocks are set on a backdrop of the World Map. Today Europe, Tomorrow ????????

CONCLUSIONS

In the introduction I stated that I was not convinced that the economy and immigration were the major issues with regard to Brexit. Over the years I have come to distrust the motives of politicians, particularly career politicians, which most now are. Following the Treaty of Nice and the Lisbon treaty I saw the EU turning much more to a political entity with the economic effort seemingly decreasing. The single market was up and running and legislation seemed to be looking at more trivial issues, Among some of the crazy facts I discovered during research was a statement that the EU criteria for materials to be used in toilet paper is 60% longer than the United Nations Declaration of Human Rights. I want less politics in my life so that I can exercise more personal responsibility.

More government, less personal responsibility

The evolution of humankind began with the hunter-gatherer. Small groups of people, probably family related members, roamed around, living on what meat they could catch and any cereal, nuts and fruit they could gather. Family size was relatively small because the logistics of continually moving determined smaller units. Any rules for living were probably made by senior family members and any discipline required administered by the same. For this they were close to the individual and could temper judgements with full knowledge of the person and events. An individual had personal responsibility to help with the work and to relate with others for the good of the whole clan.

The next stage was the development of agriculture and pastoral living. Clans settled in one place and began to husband crops and animals. This probably meant that family size increased, extended families lived together and, perhaps, were joined by other family units to form the beginnings of the village. Communal living meant extra rules and now a unit had to be formed from, again, elders, but likely now some people who were not directly related. Larger groups probably had a wise man or shaman who dispensed crude medical requirements and possibly spiritual guidance. This group living almost certainly took some of the personal responsibility from the shoulders of the individual and rested it with the ruling council. Judgements were now probably being made by unrelated individuals so less personal consideration is taken into account.

In the interest of brevity I will not detail more evolution, except to say that villages became towns, with town halls. Local government evolved with some officials in full employment and others part time. Taxes were levied to pay for the officials. Towns became cities, with mayors and deputies. Political parties filled town and city halls. With each of these steps the individual become more remote from the rule makers and enforcers, and he has to surrender more individuality for the common good of following the laws and regulations imposed.

Then we have national government, with the growing political classes. A full-time career can now be made in politics and politicians may spend more time furthering their career than administering to their constituents. Unless there is a referendum people have no direct say in events, instead they are represented by their politician. But, he, or she is more likely to toe the party line than truly represent the constituent. The politician at national level is a remote figure but, at least he may be known, if only in name, to the people he represents. Conversely the individual is, almost certainly, totally unknown to his MP. Personal responsibility has declined to an all time low and if proof of this is needed consider the following. We are told that obesity is a major problem for the future. How often do we see the headline, "What is the government going to do about it?" Smoking, drinking, drugs, gambling violent crime all have the same response – "what is the government going to do about it?" But what is the individual doing about it? For the majority the answer is, seemingly, nothing. Many individuals have given up their personal responsibility and depend upon someone else to exercise it, on their behalf, by regulation and law.

If you are asking what has this got to do with the EU? The answer is do you really want yet another layer of government, who will create many laws and regulations that supersede your national government's law? Do you want to be one individual among 508 million in the consideration of the lawmakers, or one in 66 million? Just how much are you prepared to concede? You can be an entity within a small group but if the group grows to millions are you at risk of becoming a non-entity?

Who gains most from the EU
It is frequently said that German industry and French farming are the two biggest beneficiaries form the EU. Certainly the French farming industry receives some 22% of the Common Agricultural Policy subsidy, around €9 billion per year. The German economy benefits because, effectively, it is hiding its relatively strong currency in the weaker Euro. Financial experts say that if the Euro were a stand-alone currency for Germany it should be worth as much as 20% more, against the US dollar, in terms of purchase value. Since much of the worlds trading is done in dollars it should be paying up

to 20 cents more for each dollar it spends, in other words a healthy 20% discount on purchases. This is one reason for the strength of the German economy. Secondly, when Germany was re-unified West Germany inherited the former Eastern bloc area, with its run-down infrastructure from the Communist era. Since then it has been receiving up to €18 Billion to develop these former East German States. The European taxpayer is funding this re-building of an already rich German economy.

When the EU was being formed there was a policy of sharing out the elements across the member states so that no one state was seen to have major advantage. But it was recognised that there would have to be an administrative centre. The smaller founding members, Belgium and Luxembourg, were seen to be relatively neutral and Belgium, being the larger, and with greater infrastructure was deemed to be more suitable. Since then Brussels has grown to become the de-facto capital of the EU and its prosperity has significantly increased.

Currently Belgium is the location for the Commission, the Council of the EU and the second Parliamentary seat, although second this is the more important one. The immediate financial gain can be seen from the EU's own figures for 2017 which showed that the total EU spending in Belgium was €7.358 billion. The Belgian contribution to the EU budget was €2.978 billion. Then there are the associated financial gains of having massive numbers of EU personnel and indirect associates working and living in the country. Figures indicate that 46% of the population of Brussels are non-

Belgian. Up to 60% of EU Civil Service live in the region of Brussels and some half of those have bought homes in the area. Those that are directly employed by the EU, or employed by associate representatives add up to 50,000 workers. Due to the presence of the institutions a further 20,000 people are working in Brussels and their presence is said to generate €2 billion per year. Some 2,000 foreign companies, employing 80,000 people, are also included in the population. This includes 1,200 accredited journalists, only 200 of whom are Belgian, and 10,000 registered lobbyists, whose numbers can increase to double at times of the highest political activity.

Many of the people who work in Belgium will have dependants and in Brussels there are thirty international schools to cater for the children of the expatriate community. The schools are staffed by 2.000 employees to teach some 15,000 pupils. The shops, hotels, restaurants and entertainment centres will also benefit from the large number of expatriates. A member of the Belgian parliament has commented "the prosperity of Brussels is a consequence of the European presence".

Luxembourg also hosts a number of EU organisations. Among these are the Court of Justice, Secretariat of the Parliament, the statistical office, Eurostat, the Court of Auditors, the European Investment Bank and Fund, the Publications Office and an Executive Agency for Health Agriculture and Food. These attract some 11,000 civil servants. Two European schools exist in Luxembourg and are providing education at nursery, primary and secondary levels. Like Belgium, these activities contribute significantly to the income of a country which is only 998 square mile in area (2,586 square kilometres).

The EU, direct, spending for 2017 in Luxembourg was €1.827 billion and Luxembourg, in return, contributed €0.307 billion to the EU budget.

Strasbourg is the third major city of the EU. It hosts the primary seat of the Parliament, although, as seen, this is a contentious issue. It also has the Ombudsman's office, the European Court of Human Rights and the European Youth Centre. The monthly movement of the Parliament from Brussels to Strasbourg generates a significant boost to the local income. Efforts to create a single seat parliament are blocked. Even the most recent attempt in which agencies which will be relocated from the UK, when it leaves the EU, have been suggested to move to Strasbourg, but is not sufficient to persuade Strasbourg to give up. It appears the monetary, and prestige, loss of the parliament far outweighs the gain of an agency. So, as with the other cities, there is an additional financial gain from being an EU city of choice.

For the conspiracy theorists, and some religious groups the Parliament building in Strasbourg is a sign of the EU's quest for power. It is likened to the artist Breugel's painting of the Tower of Babel. Together with an EU slogan "Speaking with one voice" this is seen by some as akin to the Biblical story in which the inhabitants of earth, who all spoke the same language, built a tower to reach to the heavens to become like God. The tower was destroyed and God scattered the people and made them speak different languages to confound further cooperation. Is this a portent of the future for the EU?

The Brexit division between young an old.
It has been said that the young are accusing the old of betraying their futures. I am not so old that I forget being young, so I can understand why this may be said. As a young man I wanted change, which I thought might be to my advantage, and I have seen many changes and I now say "be careful what you wish for". There is a saying, which has been paraphrased in different ways, that goes "If a man is not a rebel by the time he is twenty he doesn't have a heart. If he is still a rebel after he is forty he doesn't have a brain". This is the sort of generalisation we should avoid because it does not make any statement of fact. But for the young this is fact - the EU pension liability has reached €70 billion. This figure will increase, year on year, and do not forget in 2004 another 10 countries joined. In future, when retirees from all these countries become EU pensioners the liability will increase exponentially, which the young taxpayers of Europe will have to fund.

An EU report of 2015 has said that many buildings currently occupied be EU institutions are in need of repair or refurbishment – as many as 95% of buildings need some work. A new parliament building in Brussels has been proposed and the 2015 estimate for the cost was €430 million. Future EU taxpayers will have this burden to contend with. Young people, you will be faced with funding an ever increasing tax requirement for an organisation that seems to be expanding on a global scale. And, what is it doing for you? Read on.

The EU's statistical office, EUROSTAT, issued a report in 2018, which stated that 3.468 million young persons (age group 15-25) were unemployed in the EU28 and the youth unemployment rate was 15.3%. This compares to a 6.7% for overall unemployment in the EU28. Specifically the youth figures for the worst cases were Greece 36.8%, Spain 34.9% and Italy 32.5%. The figure for the UK for July 2018, for youth unemployment, was 10.9%. If I now had young children about to enter the job market I might consider those figures before voting for anything.

In February 2018 the independent EU Ethics and Science Group met to discuss the future of work. This is something that the young should be particularly interested in. Some of the points brought out in the meeting are summarised here.

- Austerity measures have led to subdued job creation and downward pressure on quality of work and employment. Both trade union density and coverage of wage agreements have declined in the European Union. Technological change (loss of routinised jobs) and globalisation (delocalisation) lead to unemployment and wage polarisation, thus exacerbating income inequalities.
- Job security and employment protection have been declining – atypical contracts and bogus

self-employment proliferated, with little or no social protection coverage. Increased employer flexibility maximises insecurity for workers, allowing for externalising risks to workers (now independent contractors rather than employees). The digital divide leads to digital exclusion. A key issue is migration – brain drain in some countries, illegal migrant labour (modern slavery) and social dumping.

When questioned, people living at the lower end of the income bands made the following points:

- PRECARIOUSNESS:"People are thrown into any kind of job, sometimes with no minimum salary and youngsters still dependent on them"
- LOW WAGES: 'Instead of saying minimum wage, we should say 'adequate' wage; we need money to live, not just to survive'
- LABOUR MIGRATION:"'Immigration caused by globalisation, capitalism, dictatorships these are dramatic situations with people becoming poorer and more vulnerable".
- GLOBALISATION:"In a global society, we need to change mindsets against a constructed scarcity of resources"
- PARTICIPATION: 'We need people to make decisions in favour of those who are falling through the cracks"
- SOCIAL PRIORITIES: "EU countries are not following up enough when it comes to social issues"

The meeting report talks of the 4th. Industrial Revolution as being the present state of industry. The first being the advent of steam driven machinery, the second was the electrification of production assembly lines and the third being the introduction of automation, made possible by IT. The fourth revolution is being driven by the technical integration of cyber physical systems and Artificial Intelligence. On this point one delegate made the point:

- The Fourth industrial revolution will not be fair by nature – as was the case with the previous ones. Previous industrial revolutions were succeeded by advances in social rights, with new labour legislation and the creation of trade unions.

The report covered the potential impact of automation and robotics on future jobs. Some of the points made follow.

- McKinsey suggests that by 2030 up to 375 million workers (14% of world's workforce by then) may need to switch jobs and learn new skills, 100 million of them in China alone. Up to one-third of the workforce in the US and Germany, and nearly half of Japanese employees, will have to learn new skills or change jobs.
- At least one-third of tasks could be automated in about 60% of jobs, which means substantial changes for employers and workers. Machine operators, fastfood workers and back-office staff are among those likely to be most affected.

- But creeping automation is unlikely to have such a big effect on jobs that involve creativity, expertise, managing people, or those that require frequent social interactions. In Germany, it is expected that digitisation and resulting automation will create 390 000 new jobs in services within the next 10 years.

Bearing in mind that this is a very recent report some of the points seem at odds with general EU proclamations regarding workers rights and protection. Great store is made of the need to remain under the cover of the EU workers charter and protection. But, the EU is firmly committed to Globalisation, which is more biased toward big business and banking. This comes back to the question, is it better to be 1 in 66 million or 1 in 508 million?

The report did not specifically cover the potential loss of jobs that automation and robotics might bring. The McKinsey report was cited, above, in highlighting the need to switch jobs, but it did not comment on losses. The study compiled by the McKinsey Global Institute, says that advances in AI and robotics will have a drastic effect on everyday working lives. In the US alone, between 39 and 73 million jobs stand to be automated — making up around a third of the total workforce. As many as 800 million jobs could be lost worldwide to automation. But, the report also states that as in the past, technology will not be a purely destructive force. New jobs will be created; existing roles will be redefined; and workers will have the opportunity to switch careers. The challenge particular to this generation, say the authors, is managing the transition. Income inequality is likely to grow, possibly leading to political instability; and the individuals who need to retrain for new careers won't be the young, but middle-aged professionals.

Developed economies like the US and Germany are likely to be hit hardest by the coming changes, as higher average wages incentivizes automation. In America, the report predicts that employment in industries like health care will increase, as society copes with an aging population; while rote jobs that involve physical labour (machinist, cooks) or data processing (payroll clerks, data entry) are most at risk of automation.

So to the young, who accuse the old of jeopardising their future by wanting to leave the political EU, I say the EU current policy seems to be more outward looking. Look only to the expansion of the EEAS activity. By focussing less on the economics and more on the politics the EU has lost its way. We need to scale down and solve the problems at home. That may be better done by leaving the political EU and pressurising national politicians into acting for the interests of the country.

A Job for life in the EU.
From the 1940's to the 1960's it was not uncommon for someone to have spent all their working life in one company or occupation. Then we were told, because of the changing nature of work and industry we could be expected to have a number of jobs during that working life, and we had to embrace social mobility and be

prepared to move locations. The EU makes it possible to have both, and move through a number of jobs within the one organisation.

To illustrate this point a random search of the EU entities stopped at the European Institute of Innovation and Technology. Its quoted mandate is to "help businesses, educational and research bodies work together to create an environment conducive for innovation and entrepreneurship in Europe". It is by no means the most significant of the institutions, but it certainly replete with titles and jargon. The following is a look at the career structure of just four of its leading staff, taken from the EIT web site.

EIT Director:
- Interim director and Chief operating officer since 2014.
- 15 years working for the EU Commission in a variety of EU posts mainly in the area of enlargement policy, having started his career with a short stint at the United Nations Economic Commission for Europe.
- Head of Operations at the EU Delegation to Serbia where he coordinated the programming and implementation of EU funds to bring Serbia closer to EU.
- Country coordinator for financial assistance for the Turkey team in the European Commission's DG Enlargement.

- In 2009, he was seconded to the Swedish Foreign Ministry in Stockholm during their EU Presidency by the European Commission.
- In 2004, he continued working on financial assistance, dealing, among other things, with the anti-corruption policies and irregularity follow-up in the use of EU funds in Bulgaria and Romania around the time of their accession.
- He started his career in the EU in Lithuania and Estonia, working in the EU Delegations and helping the two countries join the EU and ending his six years in the Baltic States as Acting Head of the EU Representation in Tallinn

EIT Head of Section
- Began her career in the Delegation of the European Commission in Prague. In this function, she was responsible for relations with civil society, academia and the Czech regions
- Worked for a Member of the European Parliament as an adviser in the fields of regional policy, justice and home affairs
- Employed by the European Commission as a Press and Communications Officer in the Directorate-General for Employment, Social Affairs and Equal Opportunities.

EIT Head of Section

- Prior to joining the EIT, he worked at the European Commission and the Research Executive Agency (REA) for more than 10 years in a variety of posts, mainly in the area of policy and project management in various units including Research Infrastructures, Research for SMEs, Research for Space and Marie Sklodowska Curie Actions (MSCA).
- Head of Operational Sector in the REA, coordinating the implementation of Horizon 2020 EU funds related to the MSCA programme, Research and Innovation Staff Exchange (RISE).

EIT Head of Strategy and Impact Unit

- Head of Strategy and Impact Unit since 1 January 2018
- Programme Officer of the Innovation Communities Unit at the EIT in April 2016 where he managed the partnership between the EIT and the EIT Raw Materials until being appointed Head of the newly created Strategy and Impact Unit.
- 15 years of experience advising EU and national policymakers and other decision makers on science and evidence based strategies, initiatives and policies on sustainable management of natural resources, resource efficiency and productivity.

This is a bewildering list of job titles and acronyms and this EU maze allows for a staggering number of job possibilities, all under the comfortable canopy of the EU. Many of the job opportunities listed on the websites state that the EU is looking for university graduates. These will enter the EU's own training academy preparatory to beginning a lifelong career in the EU.

Not only is it possible for the individual to make a career within the EU, it is also possible for family members, or even whole families to work together. The section on fraud showed that accusations of nepotism cited other family members being given jobs within an office. As for the family associations, we have the home example of the Kinnock family.

Following his failure to lead the Labour Party to election victory in 1992 Neil Kinnock was appointed to the EU commission in 1995. He held office for 10 years, until 2004, rising to become one of the Commission Vice Presidents. Later Neil was also chairman of the British Council. His wife, Glenys, was an MEP from 1994 until 2009. She employed her daughter, Rachel, as her executive assistant while working in Brussels. Son, Stephen, after graduation from University was working in the European Parliament as a research assistant. He followed this as a director in the British Council, where, coincidentally, his father was the chairman, and in 2009 he went on to become a director in something called the World Economic Forum, It should be said that these organisations are not all directly part of the EU but there are strong relationships between them.

Ironically Neil Kinnock, as a Commission VP, was put in charge of a committee to investigate corruption and nepotism and recommend reforms. During this time a Dutch MEP secretly filmed other MEP's checking in to the Parliament, to claim the €300 daily attendance allowance, before immediately leaving. Some, it was said, even left the engine of their car running to make a quick getaway. Among those filmed was Glenys Kinnock, and it was said she had done this a number of times. There is no record of any disciplinary action being taken, but, of course, the hunt was on for the person who filmed the event.

The EU Pension
Senior EU officials enjoy a pension scheme that, probably, has no equal in any other area of public service. To begin with, on leaving office they receive a payment of €300,000 to €500,000 depending on the position held. Then the pension they receive will be 70% of their final salary, and may be based upon only as little as 16 years service. For a one term office service of five or six years the pension can be as much as €5,000 per month. And, senior officials pay no contributions towards their gold plated pensions. Their, entirely free, pension scheme is entirely financed from the EU budget, i.e. the European taxpayer. And, at a time when most private companies are moving away from final salary pension schemes because they are unaffordable, the EU clings to this outdated form of pension calculation.

Is the EU really effective?

In some of the EU publicity it is often quoted that the EU, through its agencies, funds projects to the sum of €xx million. But is this really true? An examination of one agency spending can reveal some facts. This one was picked because it resonates with a major European and worldwide problem – Drugs and Drug Addiction. The EU has an Agency named the European Monitoring Centre for Drugs and Drug Addiction (EMCDDA). How much does this agency have to spend and how is it spent? The most recent annual report for this agency that contained budgetary information was 2014. This was not an easy financial report to analyse because of the jargon titles for activities but, for that year the total budget was a little under €15.2 million. This was spent as follows:

- Persons working with EMCDDA -   €9.419 million
- Support activities   €2.095 million
- Operational activities and projects   €4.32 million

The 9 million figure for persons included nearly €6.7 million for staff salaries. The rest was for pension contributions, expenses and staff extraneous costs. Support activities are things such as IT support, office requirements etc. Therefore, only €4.32 million was spent on the direct output activity and nearly three times as much spent paying staff and running the office. Browsing through annual reports for other agencies shows similar results. Is that really money well spent?

If you watch any regional news on TV from time to time you will see an item where a former drug addict, or a parent who has lost a child to drugs, have created a local initiative to try to help young people, possibly a drop-in centre where they can meet and seek help. Usually they rely on a small financial grant or local donations of money. How must the above figures appear to them? If only more of that money could be spent at local level activities.

The EU only needs some reform
When the EU attracts some adverse publicity a response is to say "we admit there are areas where change and reforms are needed". But, can it change and reform? Past history seems to cast doubts on this. Sometimes an organisation becomes so large and complex that it is difficult to introduce reform. Furthermore, the EU is an aggregation of 28 nation states which are by no means always in harmony. Even what seems to be a relatively easy reform can be blocked by national interest, as in the triple seat parliament circus. Even though 95% of MEP's would prefer a single seat parliament a national veto blocks any change. When the Institutions were described, there was the case of the Committee of the Regions and the Economic and Social Committee. Criticism from the Parliamentary Budgetary Committee, MEP's, and a parliamentary group, all calling for their abolition had no effect. Repeat instances of officials wrongly claiming allowances and cases of mal-administration are not dealt with by any form of sanction. The very head of the organisation, the Commission, fixed the appointment of the new Secretary

General in a procedure that should have attracted severe retribution, but nothing happened.

Executive agencies are only supposed to operate for specific purposes and for a prescribed time. When these were outlined the point was made that these agencies had been through many name changes. This is how the EU works to keep their peers in employment. An agency comes to the end of its allotted time. Rather than make friends, relatives and former work colleagues redundant the Commission changes the name of the agency and it continues, sometimes with an added mandate and higher budget.

Any changes to an EU treaty requires the agreement of all member states. Rising right wing parties, some with an anti-EU bias, will create problems. The EU itself, having seen how offering people a referendum, as in the Brexit case, results will be cautious in future about engaging with the people. Five referenda have been held since 2015 and all ended with the defeat of the pro-European position. The "best leave things as they are" may be the prevailing thought.

There is an adage that says "change is likely to be more successful if it comes from below". A centralized power can become blind to the need for change, fearing it might lose some of its power. In June 2018 a French-German (Meseberg) declaration suggested a framework for an EU reform programme based on consultation between governments and the Commission. There was no suggestion of input from the public. In March 2018, the

Commission produced a white paper outlining five possible futures of the EU:

- carrying on as now
- limiting the EU to the single market
- allowing the more ambitious member states to move forward (two speed Europe)
- doing less more efficiently
- doing much more together.

These options were never properly discussed in the ensuing months, as the leaders of the EU preferred to avoid a divisive debate. Two of the most pro-European figures Chancellor Merkel and President Macron have said, that "treaty reforms were possible and would have to be carefully prepared but now was not the time". And this is the problem with EU reform, even the Commission knows that reform is needed, but it is unlikely to happen, "now will never be the time". Take the second option of limiting the EU to the single market. This would mean abolishing the political elements of the EU and this is simply not going to happen. The current President of the Council of Europe was the former Prime Minister of Poland. When he took up the office of President of the Council his salary was 5 times greater than that of the Prime Minister of Poland. Add to that his expenses, privileges and pension benefits and the total package is rewarding in the extreme. In 2004 ten new countries joined the EU and eight of those were from former eastern bloc countries under the USSR. All of the officials from those countries who became part of the EU political community will have found themselves much more financially benefitted.

Take this on to the whole political community of the EU and ask, "is it likely they will agree to being made redundant in order to allow the EU to reform as only a Common Market?" In my opinion the only way this can happen is to do what the UK has done - exit the political EU. If enough countries do this there can be a return to the original idea of the Common Market. It will not happen by reform from within the current political entity. They will not give up their financial benefits or surrender their power voluntarily.

It is possible some change may come. In 2019 there will be elections for the European Parliament. It is believed that there will be a rise of nationalist and EU sceptical candidates. If these are elected to the Parliament it will change the nature of that institution. The old pro-European coalition of center-right and center-left parties may lose some or all of their authority. Changes of this sort may determine the way the EU evolves in future, but don't hold your breath waiting.

Is the EU project coming undone?
Cracks are appearing in the great EU project, Greece is subjected and held in thrall to the EU by the massive debt is has to pay back for the numerous bail-outs. In 2015 Greece suggested it might abandon the Euro currency, but the EU policy seems to say it cannot happen in isolation, leaving the currency also means leaving the group. In a 2016 poll 71% of Greeks said they had an "unfavourable view of the EU".

Italy is simmering. The EU threatens to impose sanctions because Italy wants to improve the lot of some of its people through a Budget which breaks EU financial rules. A poll taken before the budgetary dissent showed 39% of Italians see the EU as negative but how much will this increase if sanctions are imposed. The rising support for the anti-EU party "Five Star" possibly indicates that the gap between favourable and unfavourable remain is closing.

A recent survey in Sweden showed a further rise in Euro-scepticism. In 2016 a poll indicated that 54% of Swedes viewed the EU as favourable. The more recent figures indicated the gap has closed to equal, or even a move towards an unfavourable majority.

With the publicity given to Emmanuel Macron as a leading figure in the EU, particularly with respect to his arch-federalist views it might seem that France is strongly supportive. But, like some other member states the French are suspicious of the immigration policy and federal nature of the EU. The 2016 poll showed that 61% of the French now have a negative view. Together with the rise in support for right wing politicians, who express anti EU sentiments, the French position is significantly changing.

While the 2016 poll showed that 61% of Hungarians have a favourable view of the EU there have been strong clashes between the EU and the country's leader. He is strongly anti-immigration and his ruling party support him, equally strongly. If the EU forces the issue with threats of sanctions many Hungarians, who, as a nation, are strongly nationalistic, may change their minds.

In the last Czech Republic elections a Euro-sceptic party, the ODS, became the country's second largest political party. Added to this a far right, anti-European, party won 22 seats and entered parliament for the first time. The rise of the right wing in the Czech Republic, and throughout Europe, should be of concern to the EU.

It has yet to be seen what effect the exit of the UK will have on the EU. It will not be all one sided for, in some cases, the UK imports more from the EU than vice-versa. Other EU countries will suffer if a trade war ensues. If, after the UK leaves, its economy shows any signs of growth this will give ammunition to the anti-EU elements in other member states and cause problems for the EU as a whole.

If history is to be considered then a look at the other attempts to unify Europe might foretell the future. The Romans, the Holy Roman Empire, Napoleon Bonaparte and Adolf Hitler all sought, in some way, to create a unified state in Europe, and they had the force of arms to aid them. They all failed.

We must speak with a single voice.
This is one of the Mantra's of the EU. The EEAS created Embassies because it was felt that the national embassies only spoke for the narrow and independent views of the country they represented. The EU wanted a "single

European voice". But whose voice is it, the voice of Commission? The Commission is an unelected body which frequently ignores the wishes, or shapes the wishes, of it's only directly elected body, the parliament. The Meseberg declaration, in its suggested future reform stated it wanted a reduction of the number of Commissioners, even below that of the total number of member states. If that comes about some countries will lose their voice on the Commission.

When the trade agreement with Canada was being negotiated it took seven years to reach agreement with the Commission. The Commission than had to get the agreement of all member states before ratification. The Wallonia district of Belgium disagreed on one issue, so one district of one small country was able to block ratification and it took seven more months to reach that total agreement. As a result of this the President of France has suggested that some areas of policy, such as trade agreements, need not be referred to national governments and the Commission should have the authority to close deals. So by reducing the size of the Commission, circumventing the Parliament and giving the Commission absolute authority we progress toward the one voice idea, the voice of a smaller Commission.

Meanwhile back at home
Perhaps the EU should curb its outward looking activities and take a hard look at what is happening within the EU borders. While the EU, through its External Action Services is spending vast amounts of money, cultivating its external network, at home the

finances of some of its most prominent members are not so good. The national debt of the worst affected countries, as a percentage of the Gross Domestic Product for the second quarter of 2018 is shown below:

- Greece – 179.7%
- Italy – 133.1%
- Portugal – 124.9%
- Belgium – 106.3%
- Cyprus – 101%
- France – 99.1%
- Spain – 98.1%
- UK – 86.7%

Perhaps the inclusion of Belgium is surprising given the amount of direct and indirect financing it receives by being the de-facto capitol of the EU. Is it the problem of a small country trying to keep up with its larger neighbours?

By contrast some of the least indebted are among the newer member states. Romania at 34.1%, Bulgaria at 23.8% and Estonia at 8.3% are among the lowest. Is there a message to be had from this? Perhaps being a long term member of the EU, or, of the common currency, is detrimental to long term financial health.

The rise of right wing politics in Europe should be of great concern. Some say that this is partly due to EU policies of centralisation, federalisation, austerity measures and immigration policy. Immigration is one issue which is said to have influenced the outcome of the UK referendum to leave the EU. In other countries it is said to be contributory to the rise of the right. The EU leaders who defend the policy of open door immigration have little or no idea of the impact at the local levels of such a policy. In the areas in which they have their houses they are unlikely to be greatly affected. Also they have the financial means to overcome any inconvenience caused by the stretched local resources due to the influx of migrants. They might well reflect on the old proverb – "before you condemn a man you should walk a mile in his shoes".

Globalisation continually features in the EU publicity as a future aim. But what of the responsibility it brings to ensure that it is fair to all. Major corporations evade paying taxes through creative accounting. By means such as setting up fake businesses in one country, that seemingly run at a loss, and using that book-keeping loss to reduce tax liability overall. Then there are the "tax haven" countries which create favourable tax regimes for the global organisations, one country, Luxembourg being at the very heart of the EU. A recent news headline in the UK cited an, honourable, professional football player whose personal tax paid was greater than that of a number of global business giants.

Austerity, forced on countries by EU financial restrictions has hit many EU citizens. The EU criteria for a country's debts levels is that "EU member states may not have a budget deficit that exceeds three percent of their Gross Domestic Product (GDP) or a national debt that exceeds sixty percent of the GDP". The examples of national debt, previously given, show that this is exceeded by a number of countries. The EU can, seemingly in defiance of all financial logic, impose financial penalties for those outside the limits. How do you help a country in debt by adding to its debt?

A 2009 report, issued by the European Institute, gave country by country responses that showed how they would try to comply with the budget restrictions imposed by the EU. Some of these responses are shown in the following.

Greece- Budget cuts of €30 billion over three years. Public sector wage cuts up to 25 percent; lower-wage workers' bonuses capped and higher- paid workers' bonuses abolished. Non-renewal of temporary workers' contracts. VAT increase of four percent, and 10 percent increase on fuel, alcohol and tobacco taxes. Property and gambling taxes will also rise. The retirement age is set to rise by some 2 years, along with other pension cuts.

Spain- An income tax increase for those earning more than €175,000; wages cut by five percent for civil servants; 13,000 jobs will be eliminated; public investment plans to be cut by more than €6 billion. Automatic inflation-adjustments for pensions will be suspended; a baby bonus subsidy will be cut and regional funding will be cut by €1.2 billion.

France- Retirement age to rise to 62, from 60. The pay-as-you-go pension system is being raised by six months to 41.5 years of required work for full pension; a three-year freeze on public spending is being considered;

pension contributions from employees' pay will rise to 10.55 percent from 7.85 percent; income taxes for the highest income group will rise by one percent and an one-off corporate tax break will be eliminated.

Ireland- Previous austerity measures included a five percent cut in public sector wages. Capital gains and capital acquisition taxes to increase by 25 percent and cigarette tax will increase. Social welfare to be cut by €760 million and child benefits reduced by €16 per month. Investment projects to be reduced by €960 million, a new carbon tax of €15 per ton of CO_2 and a new water tax introduced.

These countries are just an example. The full report covered the then 27 member states, before Croatia joined. The report makes for sober reflection on those who have any sort of dependency on state aid. If the cuts are not directly on benefits then the cuts to social services will have the greatest effect on the least able. The emphasis on financial probity exemplifies the EU at its most uncaring for the citizen – but after all you are only 1 in 508 million. And the next time you berate the national government because of an increase in local rates, or a reduction of services, the real cause of those measures will probably be because of an EU dictate. EU national governments and banks no longer have full control, the European Central Bank and the Commission dictate the fiscal policy.

One of my favourite films is The Third Man and there is a scene where Harry Lime and Holly Martins have met at the big wheel in Vienna. Holly is berating Harry Lime for his crooked practice which has lead, indirectly, to numerous deaths. When the cabin is at its highest Harry Lime tells Holly to look down at the people below with the words "see those little dots down there Holly, how many can you count, and if one of those little dots drops down dead right now does it really matter to you old man?

The Demise of Democracy
The EU is often accused of being autocratic and lacking in democracy. We have seen how the Commission can fix appointments, as in the case of the recent appointment of the new Secretary General to the Commission. The Parliament is the only directly elected body and has no power to legislate. It can only question the Commission directives, and rather like the UK House of Lords delay the procedures. MEP's, seeking the more permanent career paths available in the EU institutions are more likely to support the Commission, who can directly, or indirectly, influence appointments. It is said that the Commission has a more subtle influence on Parliament through deals made. It is said that the Commission has an arrangement with a group of Spanish MEP's, Some Spanish members support regional independence for areas of Spain, but the Commission will not support them, in any way, if the main group of Spanish MEP's give their support, and not create problems in return. It is alleged that other such arrangements are made to keep the Parliament in check.

One course proposed for a future EU is for a single Finance Ministry, every country must join the single currency, the EU will have a single president and defence will be conducted by a single defence ministry and a single military force, an EU Army. Member states will be surrendering more of their self determination to a remote and autocratic government.

Of more concern to me is the threat to true democracy through the issue of Brexit. In 2016 a referendum was held, whose result the government of the day pledged to honour. The result was a majority vote to leave the EU. It matters not how small the majority in favour may have been, the principle of democracy is the majority decides the outcome. Any true democrat would accept that outcome, no matter how they personally voted and now felt. Any true democrat would say the majority has decided and I must now support the outcome and work together to achieve that outcome in the best way for all. Instead of which we have rancour, insult, division and opportunistic behaviour of the worst sort.

I began by saying my opinion of politicians had diminished with experience. Now it has reached an all-time low. Politicians are supposed to be the practitioners, upholders and guardians of democracy. Why didn't they say "we, the politicians, will set the example" "We will put aside party differences and work together to achieve the best outcome that fully follows the referendum result". Their division, together with the assorted remain groups, have given support and hope to the EU, who must want to see the worst possible outcome for the UK in order to discourage the rising anti EU feeling in other member states.

A true democracy would implement the result and then, if at a later stage the people wanted to change they could then do so. Democracy must be allowed to pursue its voted course if it is to be called by that name. What we now have is a group of people saying "I want democracy, but only if it agrees with my minority opinion". "If it does not agree with me I want to deny democracy and undo the result". Un-do equals Undemocratic and perhaps undemocratic people feel better if they are within the umbrella of an undemocratic organisation.

And Finally
I began this research into the EU at the time of the referendum. I was not sure what would be the best course, whether to leave or remain. As stated I was not in favour of making a decision that was based on people movement or economics. I had misgivings as I saw the EU becoming more political. When I see pictures of the grand palaces of the EU, with the flags waving, fountains gushing and with bands playing Beethoven's Ode to Joy I am not seduced. Perhaps the young would say "Wow, Great, Cool, that's for me" whereas I would say "I wonder how much that cost?"

I decided I would investigate the EU and make a decision that was knowledge based and not on sentiment and artificially induced fear of a future without the EU. I have come to the conclusion that the EU started off with good intent, the Common Market, and then lost its way. The loss happened when the politicians hi-jacked the project and set off to create a federal superstate. In reality what they have created is the greatest employment exchange for the Politicians, the Judiciary, the Bankers of Europe and the Civil Service army of camp followers. I ask you to reflect on this point - when the thousands of EU personnel turn up for a days work, not one clod of earth is turned, not one brick is laid, not one piece of metal or plastic is cut or formed, not one piece of wood is crafted, they do not pilot you in ship, aeroplane, train, bus or taxi, they do not provide you service in restaurant, shop, hotel or garage. They do nothing that is, directly, productive of any fiscal income, but they do spend and cost millions of the taxpayer provided resource. To what end, a Europe that is under severe strain, and a Europe where many are feeling, and are being, left behind.

As I write this there are riots in French cities against what they see a political elite that has no connection with its people. Perversely the left and right wings of politics rises over the ashes of burnt out cars, shops and public facilities, demanding an end to the current political rule and the creation of a new Republic. There is similar discontent in other European cities and the disparity between what the political EU says and what it actually does is part of the cause of rising discontent. I believe the EU is failing as a political entity and the political element should be stopped with a return to the original intent, an Economic Union. It is an option in the 2018

EU White paper but it will not happen from within. The Political EU must be curbed from the outside and then, perhaps it can be rebuilt as the Economic Union again.

I leave you with this final quote and comments.

> *The European Union has changed our lives for the better. We must ensure it keeps doing so for all of those that will follow us.*
> *Jean-Claude Juncker*
> *1 March 2017*

Who does he include in "our lives?" Is that the EU Presidents, Vice presidents, Commissioners, Judges, Ambassadors, Secretary Generals, Director Generals, Directors, MEP's and Special Representatives? If so that is stating the obvious, for at the end of 2018 the EU gave itself a 1.7% pay increase, backdated to July 1st, which gave Presidents an extra €5,900 per annum. He surely cannot mean the citizens of Europe who will have to work longer for less money in retirement, and who have seen their pay and pensions reduced to the point where Food Banks are proliferating. Even he cannot be that cynical – or, can he?

If there is to be another public vote, please reflect on what this "Political" European Union is doing and think long and hard before you commit pen to paper.

30970198R00084

Printed in Great
Britain
by Amazon